Data Storytelling and Visualization with Tableau

With the tremendous growth and availability of the data, this book covers understanding the data, while telling a story with visualization including basic concepts about the data, the relationship and the visualizations. All the technical details that include installation and building the different visualizations are explained in a clear and systematic way. Various aspects pertaining to storytelling and visualization are explained in the book through Tableau.

Features

- Provides a hands-on approach in Tableau in a simplified manner with steps
- Discusses the broad background of data and its fundamentals, from the Internet of Everything to analytics
- Emphasizes the use of context in delivering the stories
- Presents case studies with the building of a dashboard
- Presents application areas and case studies with identification of the impactful visualization

This book will be helpful for professionals, graduate students and senior undergraduate students in Manufacturing Engineering, Civil and Mechanical Engineering, Data Analytics and Data Visualization.

- [illegible] detailed [illegible] in Tableau [illegible] with [illegible]

Data Storytelling and Visualization with Tableau

A Hands-on Approach

Prachi Manoj Joshi and
Parikshit Narendra Mahalle

CRC Press
Taylor & Francis Group
Boca Raton London New York

CRC Press is an imprint of the
Taylor & Francis Group, an **informa** business

First edition published 2023
by CRC Press
6000 Broken Sound Parkway NW, Suite 300, Boca Raton,
FL 33487-2742

and by CRC Press
4 Park Square, Milton Park, Abingdon, Oxon, OX14 4RN

CRC Press is an imprint of Taylor & Francis Group, LLC

Library of Congress Cataloging-in-Publication Data
A catalog record has been requested for this book

ISBN: 978-1-032-30991-0 (hbk)
ISBN: 978-1-032-31035-0 (pbk)
ISBN: 978-1-003-30774-7 (ebk)

DOI: 10.1201/9781003307747

Typeset in Times
by MPS Limited, Dehradun

Contents

Preface

'You can claim your right on the work but not on the result'.

– *Bhagwad Gita*

Artificial Intelligence (AI) and Machine Learning (ML) are the buzzwords that are now heard. Their applicability is wide and they possess tremendous potential to unveil meaningful insights with analytics. Understanding the data, the patterns and the relationship is a critical factor prior to the selection, development or usage of any AI/ML approaches. So, the fundamental requirement is understanding the data and communicating effectively through it. The necessity to answer questions for the audience using the data with a story and through visualization is need of the time. This will assist the data scientists and the analysts to make potential decisions, thus addressing the Business Intelligence domain. Considering the above-mentioned factors, it is rightful to provide interested readers with a book that efficiently presents the data with a story in a wide range of impactful visualizations. With the current range of available visualization tools, one of the most powerful ones – Tableau – will help the reader to move toward effective visualizations. This will enable novice readers and researchers to know and create visualizations based on the data and their needs.

With the tremendous growth and availability of data, the book covers understanding the data, while telling a story with visualization. The book offers basic concepts about the data, the relationship and the visualizations. Through visualizations, a story is conveyed that showcases meaningful insights in the data. The book intends to provide a strong foundation in visualization to a novice reader. All the technical details that include installation and building the different visualizations are explained in a clear and systematic way. Various aspects pertaining to storytelling and visualization are explained in the book allowing the reader to gain an understanding about the importance and applicability of the topic. A book to start the journey of a budding Data Viz designer!!

This book discusses challenges involved in dealing with the data, and the need to present it in a comprehensive way. This book intends to provide a pathway to the reader from story to visualization, thereby addressing the answers required by the target audience.

The main characteristics of this book are as follows:

- Provides a hands-on approach in Tableau in a simplified manner with steps
- Numerous examples, technical descriptions and real-world scenarios
- A simple and easy language for a wide range of stakeholders from a layman to educated users, villages to metros and national to global levels
- Presents application areas and case studies with identification of the impactful visualization
- Discusses the broad background of data and its fundamentals, from the Internet of Everything to analytics
- Emphasizes the use of context in delivering the stories
- Presents case studies with the building of a dashboard
- A concise and crisp book that provides content from an introduction to building basic visualizations for the novice reader/viz designer

In a nutshell, this book displays all information (basics) that a novice and advanced reader needs to know regarding the data – its story and visualization. The book also discusses the selection and use of visualization techniques. The book also contributes to creating effective visualizations with applicability.

Data storytelling, visualizations and their applications to various branches of science, technology and engineering are now fundamental courses in all undergraduate and postgraduate courses in the field. Many universities and autonomous institutes across the globe have started an undergraduate program titled 'Artificial Intelligence and Data Science' as well as honors programs in the same subject which are open for all branches of engineering. Thus, this book is useful for all undergraduate students of these courses for a better understanding of data, its visualization, project development and product design in data science, ML and AI. This book is also useful for a wider range of researchers and design engineers who are concerned with exploring data science for engineering use cases. Essentially, this book is most useful to all entrepreneurs who are interested in starting their start-ups in the field of applications of data science to the civil, mechanical, chemical engineering and healthcare domains as well as related product development. The book is useful for undergraduates, postgraduates, industry, researchers and research scholars in Information and Communications Technology, and we are sure that this book will be well received by all stakeholders.

Prachi Manoj Joshi
Parikshit Narendra Mahalle

About the Authors

Dr. Prachi Manoj Joshi is an Associate Professor and Associate Head with the Department of Artificial Intelligence and Data Science at BRACT'S, Vishwakarma Institute of Information Technology, Pune, Maharashtra, India. She obtained her B.E. and M.Tech degrees in Computer Engineering from COEP (College of Engineering, Pune), University of Pune, India. She obtained her PhD in Computer Engineering in Machine Learning from COEP, University of Pune. She has more than 15 years of experience in academics and research. She has co-authored a book on Artificial Intelligence (PHI) and written book chapters for Research Methodology, published by CRC, and has multiple research publications to her credit. She has successfully supervised a plethora of projects for graduate and postgraduate students encompassing the domains of Artificial Intelligence, Data Mining and Machine Learning. Her research interests include Information Retrieval and Incremental Machine Learning.

Dr. Parikshit Narendra Mahalle is a senior member of the IEEE and Professor and Head of Department of Artificial Intelligence and Data Science at Vishwakarma Institute of Information Technology, Pune, Maharashtra, India. He obtained his PhD from Aalborg University, Denmark and continued as a Post Doc Researcher at CMI, Copenhagen, Denmark. He has more than 22 years of experience of teaching and research. He is a member of the Board of Studies in Computer Engineering, Ex-Chairman of Information Technology, Savitribai Phule Pune University and various universities and autonomous colleges across India. He has nine patents, more than 200 research publications (Google Scholar citations-2092+, H index-21 and Scopus Citations are 1000+ with H index-15) and has authored/edited more than 40 books with Springer, CRC Press, Cambridge University Press, etc. He is the editor in chief for the *International Journal of Rough Sets and Data Analysis,* Associate Editor for the *International Journal of Synthetic Emotions* and the *Inderscience International Journal of Grid and Utility Computing* and a member of the

Editorial Review Board for the *International Journal of Ambient Computing and Intelligence.* All these journals are published by IGI Global. His research interests include Machine Learning, Data Science, Algorithms, Internet of Things, Identity Management and Security. He is a recognized PhD guide of SSPU, Pune, and guiding seven PhD students in the area of IoT and Machine Learning. Recently, four students have successfully defended their PhDs. He has been the recipient of the 'Best Faculty Award' by Sinhgad Institutes and Cognizant Technologies Solutions. He has delivered 200+ lectures at national and international levels.

Introduction 1

1.1 INTERNET TO INTERNET OF EVERYTHING (IOE)

As stated by Mark Weiser [1], the number of devices and users connected to Internet will grow exponentially and cross 30 billion and there will be almost four devices per person on average. There has been also rapid advancement in the broadband technology over the decades resulting into high-speed and low-cost Internet with the wide availability across the globe. Today, the Internet is driving the world economy as most businesses rely on it and has also became the strongest pillar of e-commerce and m-commerce. In addition, a very large-scale integration technology is advancing at a faster rate producing the powerful processors that are equally dense. This has also contributed to improve the density to performance ratio significantly. Another key enabler is the immense transformation in semiconductor industry which has caused drastic decrease in the memory space as well as allied storage services such as cloud. It has also resulted in lowering of the cost for data storage and management. Due to advancement in high-performance computing, distribution of compute as well as processing power across multiple clusters in a decentralized manner has improved significantly. This has also enabled the faster data compute and analysis. Equally the sensor market is also improving in terms of cost and functionalities. The sensor which costs INR 100 in the year 2000, costs INR 10 in 2020, and influential use of smartphones and tablets will surely drive this market to the next level in near future.

In the sequel, the term Internet of Things (IoT) has been coined first by Kevin Ashton [2] at Auto ID lab of MIT, USA. Kevin and his team was the first to propose the global standards for Radio Frequency Identification and sensors. IoT is defined as a service and resource-constrained network which

DOI: 10.1201/9781003307747-1

connects every object, surrounding us, to the Internet. The main functionalities for anything to be connected to the Internet are sensing computing and communication functionalities. The main objective of IoT is to provide seamless and contextual services to all the stakeholders. Every IoT application consists three major components: RFID objects, sensors and smartphones [3,4]. Information and communication technology (ICT) is becoming an integral part of every use case, and today IoT is driving all these ICT-enabled use cases across the globe.

The IoT application development is advancing at a faster rate due to evolving storage platforms, sensors, programming platform and algorithmic development. It is equally important to decide some factors of IoT use case like whether it is indoor or outdoor use case, the component required to build the underlined use case, access networks required, the cost of the application, convergence technologies required and the context of the contents to be generated by the use case. Eventually the term IoT is getting transformed into the term Internet of Everything (IoE). The notion of IoE is much close to IoT where things can be users or devices and the possible interactions can be among user to user, user to device, device to device and device to user. IoE is mainly causing the data explosion and constantly changing the unit of big data. In 2015, a petabyte of data, i.e. 1024 terabytes precisely, probably met to the people definition of the big data. However, by 2025 a petabyte of data will no longer qualify as a big data at least in the enterprise. The data explosion mainly includes emails, Google searches, Facebook messages, Tweets messages and the sensory data generated by multiple IoE use cases deployed in the ecosystem. For only smart home IoT use case, allied IoT management systems are incident management system, building management system, physical access control system, video management system, GIS, HR learning management system, etc. Users, security ops and communication center are the major stakeholders for these use cases that are interacting with the IoT and outside world. The term big data and respective terminologies as well as challenges are presented and discussed in the next section of this chapter.

1.2 BIG DATA, PROPERTIES AND ANALYTICS

The big data is defined in different ways in the literature. As stated in one study [5], big data presents a type of data source that satisfies certain properties regarding the data. Prominent features which constitute four Vs of the big data are listed below:

- ***Volume:*** Deals with extremely complex and large volumes of data that essentially cannot be accommodated on the local storage and require huge remote storage on the web.
- ***Velocity:*** Deals with the data which is generated from real-time applications and the movement of data is at a high velocity of speed.
- ***Variety:*** Deals with the data collected from multisensory and heterogeneous sources
- ***Veracity:*** Deals with the important factor regarding the source of data as objectives of the data highly depends on the authenticate source of the data.

In the era of IoE, the majority of the enterprises work in Silos where main concerns are information technology infrastructure and corporate security of all the stakeholders. Diversified things, devices, objects, respective identity and access management solutions [6] and smart mobile devices which are actively participating in all the transactions are the key components contributing to the big data. In general, the data, compute and algorithms are the three main parts of any analytics. Considering the four Vs of big data, analytics on this data requires complex and proactive algorithms which can accommodate constraints like dynamic and rapid changes in the data variables (date, time of weather, sensors or customer credentials, etc.), changing patterns and the scalability. Algorithms for analytics are generally implemented in emerging programming languages such as Java, Python, R and are supported by a rich set of libraries to perform several learning operations such as machine learning, deep learning, etc. [7]. These languages are supported by active open-source communities toward regular code pupations, new ideas and customization for the underlined business problems. The traditional algorithms are different from the analytics algorithms in many ways and the difference is presented in Table 1.1.

Analysis is mainly carried out based on three approaches: descriptive analytics, predictive analytics and prescriptive analytics. Consider the example of dataset for the Bridges across India. The underlined dataset consist of different fields such as date of construction, type of bridge, type of construction, length of the bridge, material science of the bridge, etc. With respect to this example dataset, three types of analytics are explained below:

1. Descriptive Analytics

This analytics deals with the current context of the dataset. It is important to understand the past data for better understanding of the current context in terms of business intelligence. Based on the underlined dataset, the specific description of the dataset can be obtained.

TABLE 1.1 Traditional Algorithm vs Analytics Algorithms

SR. NO	*TRADITIONAL ALGORITHMS*	*ANALYTICS ALGORITHMS*
1	Accuracy depends on the algorithm	Accuracy depends on the data
2	It outputs data	It takes input as data
3	It is based on the rules	There are no rules in analytics algorithms
4	Variable values are based on statistical calculations	Variable values are based on the process of training
5	Input + Program = Output	Input + Output = Program
6	Follows mathematical approach	Follows data-oriented and data-intensive approach
7	The orientation is on interpretation	The orientation is on prediction
8	E.g. Bubble Sort Algorithm	E.g. Classification or Clustering

Example: How many times the bridge was repaired during the period of 2018 to 2021?

2. Predictive Analytics

It uses analytics algorithms based on the learning techniques by anticipation process. In this analytics, the patterns and anomalies are studied and used for the prediction purpose and to draw more meaningful insights as well as inferences. The main objective of predictive analytics is to look into the future for better business perceptive.

Example: How many bridge accidents are likely to occur in next two years?

3. Prescriptive Analytics

This analytics works on the outcome of predictive analytics and provides set of recommendations in order to improve more on the business intelligence. This analytics helps to answer the question of the form 'What should be done?', 'What can we do for ….?', etc.

Example: In above example if the predictive analytics is giving predictions of two accidents. Then prescriptive analytics suggest what can be done so that in next two years there will be no bridge accidents.

The main success of any analytics algorithm is based on your understanding about the data pertaining to the given problem. In addition to this, the accuracy of predictions and forecasting highly depends on the type of data, errors in data and faults in data.

Business decisions are generally made on dynamic and constantly volatile data coming from a variety of sources. The two main sources of the data are as follows:

- *Internal Data:* This includes the record data from traditional applications such as customer details, health records, payroll data, finance-related data, etc.
- *External Data:* This includes the data from external sources such as mobile data, news feeds, data from online social networks, metrological data, geographical data, etc.

The data structure used to store and analyze data also plays a crucial role in data analytics. Structured data are stored in the form of rows and column and use relational databases as a storage platform for processing. In structured data, the dimensions, format, and type are known in advance and enterprises have lot of structured data locally stored on the servers. This type of data includes the data collected from sensors in IoT environments, data collected from the activity log in web computing, logistic data in the process of sales, data from the financial and insurance domain, weather data, etc. On the other side, unstructured data do not follow any specific format but it has a typical implicit structure. Storage, processing and analysis of these unstructured data is a big challenge and data scientists have lot of opportunities in this area for revenue generation. Industry 4.0 and emerging trends such as cloud computing, mobile and wireless communication and online social media are the key enables for the unstructured data. These data include data from online social media, phone data, images from satellite, all images and videos from various use cases. In addition, data governance is another important criterion for the execution of analytic algorithm to solve real-world business problems. We also need to define and inculcate the required skills for the efficient application of analytics on the underlined data. These skills are listed below.

a. **Availability of Tools**

There is a diversified scope for applications of tools in data analytics. Application of these tools varies from the type and other characteristics of data. Series of experimentations, application of different approaches and tools on data to solve real-world problem, exploring design issues of various open-source or license tools are some initial steps required to impart the process of analytics.

b. **Language Selection**

Due to advancement and transformations in the field of programming languages, varieties of options are available for programmer and data scientist to explore. It is important to understand emerging programming languages (Python, R, Java, C++), allied tools (Linux, Spark, Hadoop), storage services, their advantages, limitations and their application to underline analytics problems.

c. **Algorithm Selection**

Understanding the given analytics problem, its objective and set of questions to be posted on the dataset to solve problem and selection of appropriate algorithm are the main steps in analytics. Algorithms for pattern matching correlation, classification, clustering, detection and identification are few of the available options for data scientists.

d. **Model Selection**

For making sense out of big data and drawing meaningful insights, selection of appropriate model and building it is one of the crucial steps. Recent Application Program Interfaces such as TensorFlow, Spark enable model building and training more efficient. Use of correct methodology such as federated learning [8], relevant libraries, mapping of dataset to the type of algorithm with respect to design issues plays an important role in obtaining the outcomes.

e. **Impact of Probability and Statistics**

The main objective of analytics algorithms is to deal with the problems having uncertain nature and outcome is to predict, forecast, estimate, etc. These algorithms and their basic implementation is based on the probability and statistical theory. Analyst must have fundamental knowledge of these mathematical concepts in order to improve and enhance application development in analytics. Regression, Hidden Markov Models are some examples of algorithms based on these principles [8,9].

f. **Data Management**

Analyst and data scientist have to understand data across all verticals which includes data source, data reliability, ownership, etc. End-to-end management of the underlined data pertaining to the given problem plays an important role in entire data processing.

g. **Data Source**

Authenticity and cleanliness of the data source is highly connected to the success or failure of analytics algorithm. Data cleaning is next important step which involves the removal of noise, unwanted fields, duplicate values and missing values. Understanding data and different use cases from pilot to real production environment helps to gain more insights on the process.

In addition, General Data Protection Regulation (GDPR) [10] proposes the rules and norms to be taken care particularly when the enterprise or personal data are being handled for processing and analysis. Data governance also includes deployment of required security provisions, unauthorized access, compromising data, privacy of sensitive data, principle of least privilege and selective disclosure. The next section elaborates on various issues and challenges related to the data analytics.

1.3 ISSUES AND CHALLENGES

Data analysis and application of learning algorithms is gaining lot of popularity and global acceptance due to increasing data size. Business processes are also driven by machine learning techniques for better anticipation in business intelligence. All these processes are data intensive and algorithms used to run resource-constrained mobile and IoT devices. Issues and challenges with data analytics and application of learning algorithms are as follows:

- **Scale**
  Large number of users, devices and their ubiquitous nature is transforming the scale of data. IoE, IoT, cloud, artificial intelligence and their integration enable large and fast-growing data across all the verticals. Size and complexity of the data has become a problem, and old way of processing data doesn't work effectively on this big data. The issues related to the big data such as storage, movement, loading and transforming are now absolute. However how to explore and analyze this big data and how to process this data in order to draw meaningful insights are the main issues being faced by all IT leaders.
- **Pace**
  Real-time analytics, fast pace analytics, commanding and controlling the data with high pace are other daunting issues in analytics and processing. We require customized skills to carry out data science and high-performance computing platforms as well as learning-aware platforms to process the data.
- **Environment**
  Complex infrastructure deployed for IoT and IoE, different integrations platforms and framework for cloud and big data add

more complexity to the environment. Vulnerability analysis [11] shows that there are more security and privacy requirements for such complex environments with the features such as alerts management, real-time monitoring, log tracking, etc. This challenge also affects the application of appropriate algorithms and techniques for data processing.

- **Data Preparation and Training**
  For application of analytics and cognitive techniques on the data, data preparation and its training is one of the most important challenges. The data collection, preparation and labeling is the first step to be carried out by data scientists or they can also use datasets from the repositories and use widely accepted tools to prepare and label it. These options completely depend on the enterprise and the methodology adapted by the policies of organization. Application of cognitive and analytics model works in offline and online modes. In most of the cases these models are offline where initially prepared data are used to train the model and same model is used for the different purposes. This mode assumes that the further incoming data will be consistent as it was while training the model initially. However, this ideal situation does not remain constant for all the use cases and subsequently offline model fails. For more accurate predictions and forecasting, online models are preferred where retraining of the data is required. Retraining data is another important challenge in this process in order to address the pace and changes in the data.
- **Specialized Hardware**
  In nutshell, analytics, cognitive, machine and deep learning models are designed and developed to process big data. Implementation and execution of these models requires high-performance computing platform and specialized hardware. Availability of such high-end configuration with the processing and storage capabilities is important bottleneck. Fortunately, due to advancements in hardware industry, procurement of such facility is becoming affordable. The use and importance of GPU and CUDA for deep learning and field-programmable gate arrays for machine learning is gaining more popularity due to commendable results.
- **Trust**
  Trust in communicating with data and communicating data are equally important from the perspective of developer and end user. In critical applications such as healthcare, military applications, clinical decision support systems, construction management in civil engineering trust on the results produced by different models play a crucial role.

- **Transparency**
  Maintaining transparency during data preparation, training, model building processing and application of different algorithms is crucial step. Explainable artificial intelligence [12] is one of the important steps toward maintaining the transparency. Explanation of the outcomes and results produced by different models creates more impact and brings more value to the process.
- **End-to-End Processing**
  End-to-end process for commercial applications is highly appreciated by all the stakeholders. End users are more interested to look at the product as overall process instead of separating the role into development to deployment to operations. The products are also to be developed by considering end-to-end processing factor from the design phase.

1.4 CONCLUSION

This chapter presents the notion of IoT and IoE in the view of big data and discusses the various factors responsible for increasing data. Different issues in data analytics and difference between traditional algorithms and analytics algorithms are presented and discussed in the next part of this chapter. Different types of analytics with example and skills required for performing better analysis are also discussed in this part. Finally this chapter concludes with the various issues and challenges in the analysis process.

REFERENCES

1. Parikshit N., Mahalle and Sheetal S. Sonawane. *Foundations of Data Science Based Healthcare Internet of Things*. Springer Singapore, 2021.
2. Kevin Ashton. That 'Internet of Things' Thing, *RFID Journal*, 22 June 2009.
3. Parikshit N., Mahalle and P. N. Railkar. *Identity Management for Internet of Things*. River Publishers, Wharton, TX, USA, 2015.
4. Parikshit N., Mahalle. Identity Management Framework for Internet of Things, PhD Dissertation: Aalborg University, Denmark, 2013.
5. Machine Learning For Dummies®, IBM Limited Edition Published by John Wiley & Sons, Inc. 111 River St. Hoboken, NJ 07030-5774 www.wiley.com Copyright © 2018 by John Wiley & Sons, Inc.

6. P. N. Mahalle, B. Anggorojati, N. R. Prasad and R. Prasad, Identity Driven Capability Based Access Control (ICAC) Scheme for the Internet of Things, 2012 IEEE International Conference on Advanced Networks and Telecommunications Systems (ANTS), 2012, pp. 49–54.
7. Bengio, Y., Courville, A. and Vincent, P., 2013. Representation Learning: A Review and New Perspectives. *IEEE Transactions on Pattern Analysis and Machine Intelligence*, 35(8), pp. 1798–1828.
8. Khadse, V.M., Mahalle, P.N. and Shinde, G.R., 2020. Statistical Study of Machine Learning Algorithms Using Parametric and Non-Parametric Tests: A Comparative Analysis and Recommendations. *International Journal of Ambient Computing and Intelligence (IJACI)*, 11(3), pp. 80–105.
9. Machine Learning, Tom Mitchell, McGraw Hill, 1997.
10. The Proposed EU General Data Protection Regulation. A guide for in-house lawyers, Hunton & Williams LLP, June 2015, p. 14.
11. C. Panchal, V. M. Khadse and P. N. Mahalle, Security Issues in IIoT: A Comprehensive Survey of Attacks on IIoT and Its Countermeasures, 2018 IEEE Global Conference on Wireless Computing and Networking (GCWCN), 2018, pp. 124–130.
12. Yu-Liang Chou, Catarina Moreira, Peter Bruza, Chun Ouyang, and Joaquim Jorge. 2021. Counterfactuals and Causability in Explainable Artificial Intelligence: Theory, Algorithms, and Applications. arXiv:cs.AI/2103.0424

Data Storytelling 2

2.1 OVERVIEW

The main objective of data storytelling is to enable users about understanding context of the data, learning different approaches to gain insights on the data and then enabling transformations of these insights into story building and its presentation. There are different roles in data analytics which include data analyst/developer/DBA, data scientist/decision scientist and business intelligence developer. The responsibilities of these specific roles are described below:

1. **Data analyst/developer/DBA:** Collecting data in various formats, data cleaning, data formatting and converting underlined data to the particular formats.
2. **Data scientist/decision scientist:** Taking these data in a statistical tool, performing data exploring and data analysis, running statistical models on this processed data and then finally converting output in the desired formats.
3. **Business intelligence developer:** Taking above output in the reporting tool such as Microstrategy or Tableau, preparing visualization reports, optimizing these reports and then communicating reports with the customers.

Data generation is a method of applying preprocessing to data for data preparation and once the data are ready then we apply different techniques and algorithms to extract knowledge which is used for business intelligence. Associating context with the data for better insights and performance metrics finalization for better efficiency are the main objectives of data storytelling.

Consider the digit 57. If the question posted you to answer what is this digit 57? There will be variations in the responses like it is a number, it is a value.

DOI: 10.1201/9781003307747-2

However, unless and until we do not associate context with this number it will have no meaning. In practice, it can be the roll number of any student, it can represent the age of person, it can be marks or percentage, it can be price of some item, it can be the lane number in home address, etc. Association of the context with 57 has given meaning to it. Initially always the data are raw and association of the context and processing to these raw data provide information. From this processed information, the knowledge is extracted which is used for the business purpose. Knowledge always targets some purpose with the underlined data, and making this knowledge presentable and communicable to the end user is also equally important. Visualization plays a vital role by selecting the right graph for right data and is explained in Chapter 3 of this book. In brief, the important terms in this process are discussed below and presented in Figure 2.1:

- **Data:** Present the discrete elements such as words, numbers, codes, tables, etc.
- **Information:** Presents the linked elements such as sentences, paragraphs, concepts, etc.
- **Knowledge:** Presents the actionable information such as theories, chapters, stories, etc.
- **Wisdom:** Presents the applied knowledge such as books, poetry, philosophies, etc.

In addition to the paradigm presented in Figure 2.1, analytics process follows few important steps which are listed and explained below:

Data Identification: Data identification for the underlined problem and analysis of various sources where the required data are available is the first step in the process. It is also possible that the data available initially is very small and the provision is also to be made for data expansion to improve the outcomes.

Data Preparation: The next step is to prepare the data for analytics which includes data cleaning (missing values, inconsistent data and outliers),

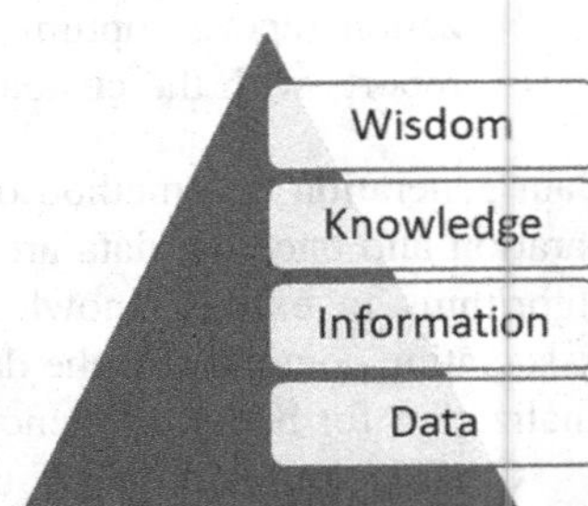

FIGURE 2.1 Knowledge Paradigm.

integration (aggregating/federating data from multiple sources), transformation (scaling up and down) and reduction (dimensions).

Algorithm/Technique Selection: Selection of an appropriate algorithm for a given dataset and given problem is another important step. Selection of the algorithm and technique also depends on the business challenge we need to address.

Model Building: Training and retraining of the growing data, deciding the strategy for model building is the key step in the process.

Evaluation: The next step comprises the evaluation of model for various performance metrics in order to find optimal and outperforming algorithm.

Deployment: The developed model then needs to be deployed at local storage or the remote storage and this mode highly depends on the scalability (numbers of users and devices) of underlined applications.

Analyze: The next step is to analyze the outcomes based on the requirements and constraints incorporated in training, algorithm and techniques.

Assessment: Assessment is the last step in the process where quality and validity of the analysis is measured. The information collected after this assessment is then used as a feedback to improve the performance.

Figure 2.2 presents this entire process as cycle:

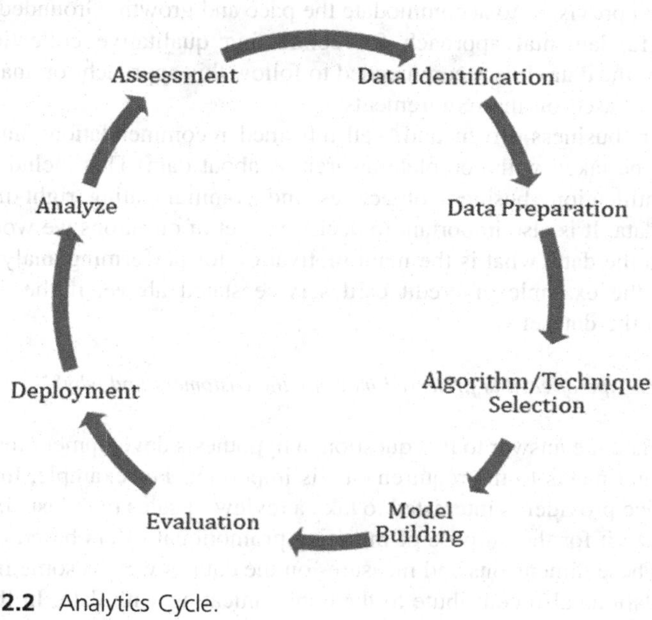

FIGURE 2.2 Analytics Cycle.

2.2 COMMUNICATING WITH DATA

Communicating with data requires a pool of fundamental necessary skills. This section elaborates more on these skills and also presents some examples to demonstrate these skills. Consider the example of credit card service provider organization that is responsible for providing different types of end-to-end credit card services to banks, financial organizations, corporate and individual customers in the varied range. Credit card service provider has different verticals such as management, issuer, sales, rewards, recovery, legal, etc. and all these sectors are available with the abundant of data from the past, and the first important challenge is to communicate with these data for better business intelligence. In this context, the data available for every sector are different with different domain parameters. Finding similarities and differences to draw concepts and reflection for establishing the association helps to communicate with these data more effectively. Identification of regularities by applying 'divide and conquer strategy' by dividing data into smaller parts/ more meaningful units is also important. Forming category of these data by inductive process and refining these categories for conceptual understanding, negative evidences and pattern discovery is also required. These categories and pattern discovery are subject to change with the growing data and there should be a provision to accommodate the pace and growth. Grounded theory [1] is a fundamental approach for conducting qualitative collection and analysis of the data. It is recommended to follow this approach for analysis of the dataset based on the requirements.

Faster, business-driven and well-informed recommendations and decisions can be taken with complete awareness about data. This includes audience identification, business objectives and communicating right message with the data. It is also important to decide the set of questions we would like to post on the data, what is the main motivation for performing analysis, etc. Consider the example of credit card service stated above, if the question posted on the dataset is

'Which type of card is preferred more by the customers and why?'.

To formulate the answer to this question, a hypothesis development that fits to the data and meets to the requirements is important. For example, the credit card service provider is interested to take a review of sales over last six weeks and analyze it for the purpose of initiating promotional offers based on some criteria. These dimensions and measures on the data as well as some filters on the calculations also contribute to the communicating with data. In the same example, consider that the review of the sales for a particular type of card and for a particular type of customers is required. In such cases, the filters on the dataset can be used to answer this question by associating priorities to certain fields or attributes. The same example can also be extended where the analysis is to be carried out only to the customers availing credit card service since last one year. In the sequel, timeliness is also one of the important factors for communicating with data. Analysts are recommended to confirm the set of these components in order to communicate with data more effectively. The outcomes of any analytics and data science project are always technical and difficult to make them communicable. Data understanding, interpretation, generating story out of these data and presenting it to the well-identified audience are the main pillars in communicating with data. Based on the descriptive statistics, building predictive and prescriptive models with more justification on the conclusion is the next step of this process. Explanation of the outcomes and its justification in terms of explainable AI [2] is becoming more popular particularly in the context of critical applications such as healthcare, emergency monitoring, etc. The language of data through data storytelling and designing different graphs to tell a story are two main parts which are explained below.

- **Storytelling**

Data storytelling is the essential skill that every data scientist needs to possess. Understanding business context for data ingestion, understanding end-user requirement; answering the questions like why, what and how? and delivering personalized data to individual through visualizations by answering questions posted on the data are the main steps in data storytelling. The basic questions before we start on our story are as follows:

1. ***Who are you writing for?***

Whether these are presented to the CEO or Project Manager or the Team lead of the project or also may be to the customer/user.

2. ***What are you trying to communicate?***

Deciding on what part and features of the data we are interested to present.

3. ***Why is this important?***

Motivation for shaping the story explains why it is so important.

Consider the healthcare use case where the actors are patient and doctor. During the first visit with doctor, the obvious question posted to patient is related to the symptoms and statistics regarding physiological parameters, past medication and past disease history. This phase is referred as a descriptive phase. Based on the analysis of data collected from this phase, then doctor generally recommends and prescribes some medical test to be carried out for the purpose of next-level analysis and this phase is referred as diagnostic phase. After this descriptive phase (past) and diagnostic phase (present), doctor makes some predictions about the occurrence of some physiological parameters in the future and this phase is referred as predictive phase. Based on these virtual predictions doctor then converts these virtual predictions into actionable elements by writing some medicines and tablets to the patient and this phase is known as a prescriptive phase. This process clearly tells that based on the timeline analysis of past, present and future, doctor is able to perform this prescriptive analysis being a domain expert. These are the four pillars of any data science process irrespective of the underline application and are depicted in Figure 2.3.

Data storytelling is not the application of data science phases described above but it also consists of the decision on which type of learning we apply to build the model, which algorithm from particular learning method is more appropriate for the data, which tool is more useful for building the stories, etc. Tools are very important in data storytelling and data science but technique is everything in the entire process. There should be some library support or automated intelligent approach which can find out missing values, command lie approach to clean the data proactively, automate the process of preprocessing the data, audit the data quality as well as pattern discovery from the underlined data.

Data storytelling is very important for attending interviews for data science or whenever you are doing some data science project in any company because there are many stakeholders to whom you will be actually communicating and you need to do a lot of analysis for this. A good data story must be a combination of three main elements which include data, narrative and visualizations and they must complement each other. The exploratory and explanatory are the main two states of data storytelling. In exploratory state,

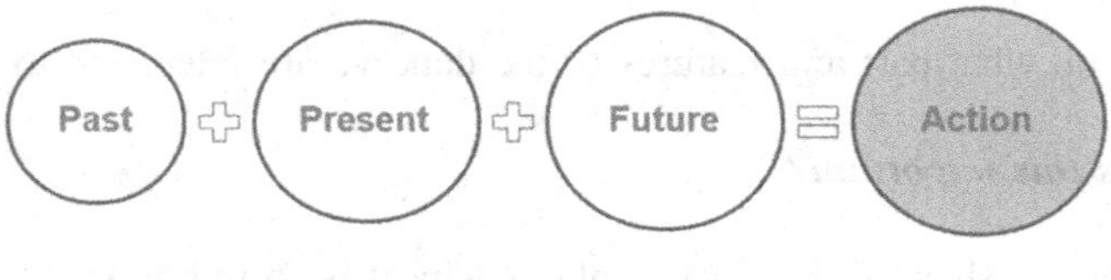

FIGURE 2.3 Data Science Phases.

getting familiar with the data and having insights on the outcomes are the main tasks. In explanatory state, communicating data to the audience who are not familiar with your findings is the main task and it can be accomplished with simplicity, clarity and cohesion. The good data story should contain the following six main components:

1. **Data foundation:** Preparing data for storytelling is very important aspect in storytelling being the main building block. There should be good amount of qualitative and quantitative data available for the processing.
2. **Main point:** Entire data storytelling should have a central idea and purpose insight for presenting the story to drive change.
3. **Explanatory focus:** Knowing your audience is very important in the storytelling part. Audience should be able to interpret the data based on the methods and motivation. Audience also should be able to address and understand why and how of the data story.
4. **Linear sequence:** Data story must have a linear sequence for understanding of the patterns in the data as well as storytelling part.
5. **Dramatic elements:** The presence of a dramatic element in the data story makes story more convincing.
6. **Visual anchor:** Visual effects and presentation help audience to see trends, patterns and anomalies in the data more easily and it also helps for tailoring our presentation.

- **Data Visualization**

Data visualization include presenting our data using visual components such as graphs, charts which are generated from the dataset available in different forms such as spreadsheet, tables, comma-separated values, etc. Communicating the substance of data and their metrics in the data is the main focus of visualization to provide clear context of the data, holding attention to the key insights of data, and in turn, leading to certain useful actions. Essentially, good data visualization must address the following eight main points.

1. **Communicating with data:** The language of data for clear understanding and effective communication is very important. In addition to this, the context of the data and purpose should be very clear for effective visualization.
2. **Good and bad data visualizations:** Factors responsible for making good visualizations and reasons for making bad visualizations needs a detailed thought process before preparing the visualizations.

3. **Communicating visually:** Visual perception which includes order, hierarchy, clarity, relationship, convention and visual design creates more impact on the better visualizations.
4. **The right graph for the right data:** Available component for visualization in the underlined tool or framework, category of the data and right graph for the right data create more impact on the visualization. Deadly sins of graph, avoiding being misled by data are some of the important points to be taken care of.
5. **Designing graph to tell a story:** Clearing clutters from the visualizations and bringing out the story with different colors play a vital role in data storytelling with visualization.
6. **Craft an impactful data narrative:** Analytics value chain, data narratives, turning visualizations into actual story are important points for crafting impactful narratives.
7. **Bringing it all together:** Finally what is your main point and objective, picking your right visualization, editing it for clarity if required, formatting it for more impact, formatting it for narrative are few main steps for bringing it all together in nutshell.

2.3 STORYTELLING CONTEXT

Context association with the data and storytelling is applicable to end-to-end process from data to outcome and the main questions to be addressed are presented and discussed below.

1. **How did this initiative come about?**

The main goal, objectives and the purpose of entire initiative should be addressed through this question during the process.

2. **What would you consider a successful answer?**

During storytelling, many questions are posted on the data and the main objective is to find answers of these questions through analytics. The performance matrix needs to be defined for considering answer as a successful answer.

3. **Do you have any suspicions about the data?**

Suspicions about data, any concerns regarding the source, nature, type, etc. should be raised before we start the process.

4. **What specific things should I investigate?**

The key components to be investigated in data storytelling for more meaningful insights are very important.

5. **How do we measure a successful outcome?**

There should be well-defined upper and lower thresholds for the performance measures in data storytelling.

6. **What potential actions/outcomes could come of this?**

Issues, challenges, outcomes and learning should be well defined well in advance in order to answer this question.

7. **How does this contribute to your business?**

How outcome will contribute to the business intelligence need to be defined well in advance.

8. **What are the main key performance indicators (KPIs) of your business, and how does this relate?**

KPIs of the underlined business and their relation with the outcomes of data storytelling are very important.

9. **What are potential threats or opportunities I should be aware of?**

SWOT analysis needs complete attention during the process for better and useful outcomes from the analysis.

10. **Is there anything within the data I should not look for?**

Few characteristics and features of the data can be overlooked if they are not in the interest of underlined business problem.

2.4 CASE STUDIES

This section presents and discusses important case studies with sample dataset in order to give readers complete insights into the data storytelling and visualization aspects. These case studies provide the description of the problem statement and the probable solution.

CASE STUDY 1 DATA STORYTELLING

PROBLEM STATEMENT

Create a data story that shows which of the three cinemas has the most successful concession stand.

TASK

Review the data and context provided and prepare an impactful data communication that effectively tells the story of which of the three cinemas has the best performing concession stand.

The data are provided in Excel – but you can use any tool you are comfortable with to prepare the story.

Tip – Review the context of the communication to understand what determines the most successful concession stands among three cinemas.

RESOURCES

Below you will find the Excel sheet that contains four tables.

1. The number of tickets sold for each of the three cinemas for the three months.
2. The price each of the cinemas charges for the items they sell at the concession stand.
3. The monthly sales number and revenue for each of the items each cinema sells at the concession stand.
4. Cinema ID Key table.

This project deals with a theatre namely Light Speed Cinemas whose owner wants to figure out best cinema among these three cinemas. Also, he is interested in knowing what factors made it the best. The theatre has collected data from past three months such as the number of tickets, number of sales and the total revenue generated. These data are presented to us in the form of an excel sheet as shown in Figure 2.4.

Next, you will find meeting notes taken from a meeting with the management of Light Speed Cinemas. The following questions were asked to understand the context.

Month	Cinema	tickets
Feb-19	1	27034
Mar-19	1	29301
Apr-19	1	31269
Feb-19	2	22775
Mar-19	2	21465
Apr-19	2	24138
Feb-19	3	42546
Mar-19	3	39490
Apr-19	3	38093

Cinema	Product	Cost
1	Popcorn	$ 4.50
1	Soda	$ 2.80
1	Candy	$ 2.60
2	Popcorn	$ 4.20
2	Soda	$ 3.50
2	Candy	$ 2.85
3	Popcorn	$ 4.00
3	Soda	$ 3.15
3	Candy	$ 2.49

Cinema
1
2
3

Month	Cinema	Produc	Sales Number	Sales Rev
Feb-19	1	Popcorn	18342	82539
Feb-19	1	Soda	17340	48552
Feb-19	1	Candy	4245	11037
Mar-19	1	Popcorn	19304	86868
Mar-19	1	Soda	16790	47012
Mar-19	1	Candy	3784	9838.4
Apr-19	1	Popcorn	17422	78399
Apr-19	1	Soda	15308	42862.4
Apr-19	1	Candy	5688	14788.8
Feb-19	2	Popcorn	19981	83920.2
Feb-19	2	Soda	17330	60655
Feb-19	2	Candy	5668	16153.8
Mar-19	2	Popcorn	18034	75742.8
Mar-19	2	Soda	16873	59055.5
Mar-19	2	Candy	5088	14500.8
Apr-19	2	Popcorn	18930	79506
Apr-19	2	Soda	16490	57715
Apr-19	2	Candy	5366	15293.1
Feb-19	3	Popcorn	25099	100396
Feb-19	3	Soda	22834	71927.1
Feb-19	3	Candy	8409	20938.41
Mar-19	3	Popcorn	26711	106844
Mar-19	3	Soda	23940	75411
Mar-19	3	Candy	8790	21887.1
Apr-19	3	Popcorn	25873	103492
Apr-19	3	Soda	22098	69608.7
Apr-19	3	Candy	7804	19431.96

FIGURE 2.4 Resources for Case Study 1.

Subject: Analysis to understand which cinema has the most successful concession stand.

Question: Which of the three cinemas do you believe is performing the best?
Answer: I'm unsure – perhaps it is the one that sells the products for the highest price.

Question: What do you mean by a successful concession stand?
Answer: The one that sold the most product.

Question: How does selling the most products fit into the business's objectives? Could you provide some background?
Answer: We don't have any say on what types of movies are made, how they're advertised and how audience will review them – we can only sell tickets to whatever movie is out. Whenever we sell a ticket, a large portion of it goes to the movie studio and then from what is left, considering the cost of running the cinema, profit margins on ticket sales are slim. So the main revenue we generate is from the concession stand. Our objective is to maximize revenue at the concession stand for each ticket sold.

Question: Is there any specific questions I should investigate within the data?
Answer: Yes, I want to understand which cinema generates the most revenue per customer at the concession stand.

Question: So what would a good presentation look like to you?
Answer: If I could clearly identify which cinema was the best, and what factors made it the best, then that would be a great presentation.

Solution: The study of the sale at concession stands is as important as studying the sale of tickets. The descriptive statistics derived from the given data is as follows.

Figure 2.5 clearly shows the numbers of tickets sold were maximum for the cinema 3 and was around 120000 tickets cumulatively for all the three months. This figure also shows the sales of the number of items sold by a particular cinema cumulatively for all the three months. It clearly shows that the number of sales for the third cinema was the highest i.e. 171558 items. So it is concluded that since the number of tickets sold were maximum in cinema 3, the number of items sold were also maximum in cinema 3.

Figure 2.6 shows overall revenue generated by the three cinemas cumulatively in the past three months. It clearly shows that the overall revenue generated from the third cinema is maximum, that is $589936.27. The graphs depicted in Figures 2.5, 2.6 and 2.7 make it crystal clear that cinema 3 clearly outperforms the other two cinemas since the number of customers who approached it was also the maximum. This result is very obvious and hence no clear conclusion could be drawn from it. In the sequel, it would be good idea to calculate a unique value 'Revenue per ticket' to be able to compare between different cinemas. Figure 2.7 shows that the revenue generated per ticket is highest for second cinema and has completely outperformed the others. As we can see in the figure the difference between the revenue per ticket of the second cinema is almost 2 units greater than the other two cinemas i.e. about $6.76.

The very first point that made Cinema 2 shine is its sharp cost assignments. The most important and traditional thing to buy on a concession stand is popcorn. In cinema 2, the price of popcorn was cleverly averaged to unwillingly force the customers to buy it. On the contrary, the prices of soda and candy which are most likely to be bought alongside the popcorns were sharply increased. This maximized the total cost of the three together. The customer who buys popcorn at a fair rate is most likely to buy other things at a moderately high rate. Figure 2.7 shows the average price of the three items bought together. This average price stayed constant throughout the period of three months and clearly states that the highest average price per package of three was for second cinema and was about $3.52.

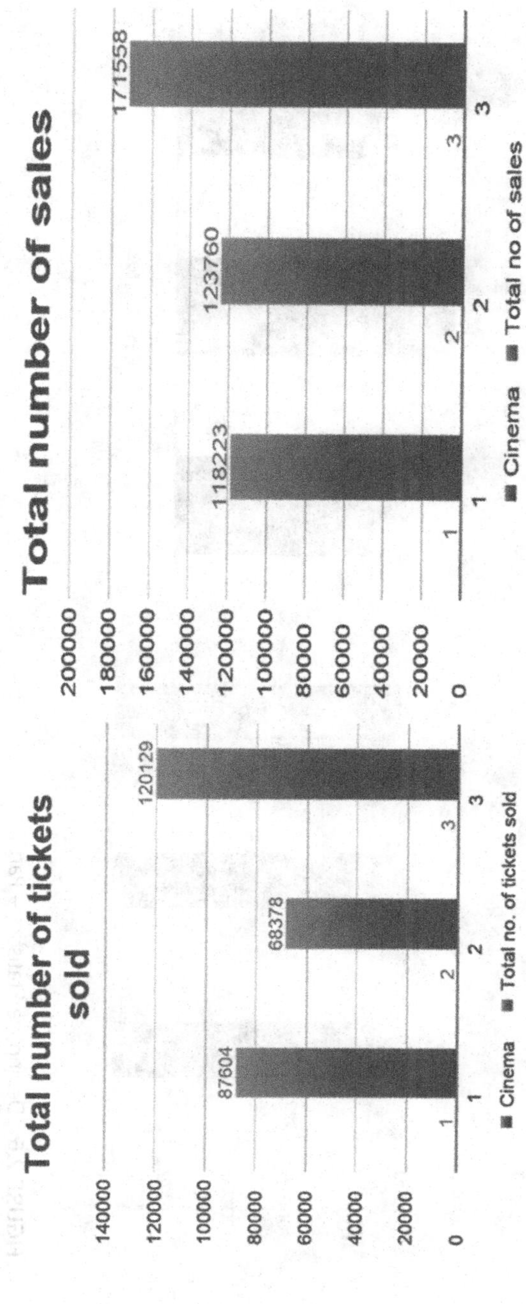

FIGURE 2.5 Descriptive Statistics – Part I.

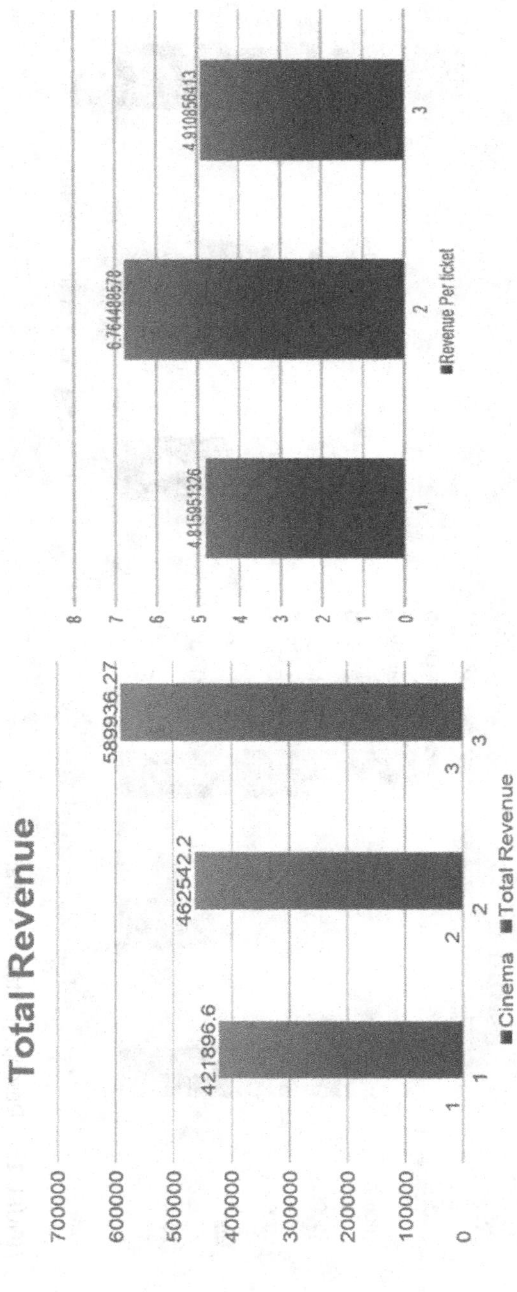

FIGURE 2.6 Descriptive Statistics – Part II.

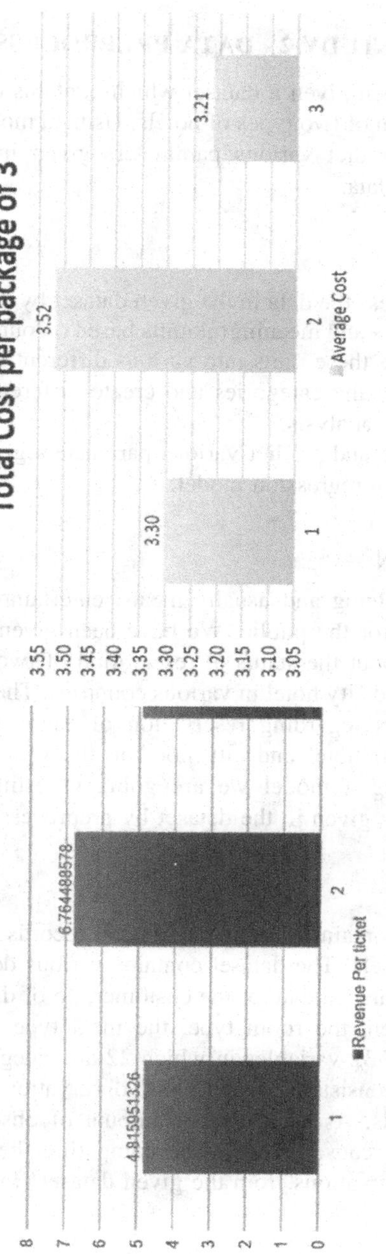

FIGURE 2.7 Storytelling – Cinema.

CASE STUDY 2 DATA PREPROCESSING

Brief: We have been given a dataset which contains details about the status of reservation of two types of hotels. Using a model we are going to estimate and predict various parameters given in the dataset by preprocessing the data.

TASKS

- To preprocess the data in the given dataset by dividing it into smaller units and meaningful units based on our major points.
- To organize these units into various different categories.
- To compare the categories and create different patterns for further data analysis.
- To estimate and predict various parameters given in the dataset using a regression model.

INTRODUCTION

Hotel provides lodging and usually meals, entertainment and various personal services for the public. We have been given a dataset which contains details about the status of reservation of two types of hotels, viz, resort hotel and city hotel in various countries. The dataset contains various parameters regarding reservation of each and every person living in the resort hotel and city hotel in the year 2015 and 2017, respectively. Using a model we are going to estimate and predict various parameters given in the dataset by preprocessing the data.

RESOURCES

The raw dataset contains various details and records of the customers residing in the hotels. The dataset contains various details such as the type of hotel, the arrival date of the customer, no of days of stay, no of adults and children, the room type, the meal type, etc. Our dataset contains a total of 32 variables in which 22 are categorical and 10 are numeric. Also it consists of over 120000 observations combining both the types of hotels. As such a large amount of observations are not required and may cause errors while computing the code, we select random 3000 observations from the given dataset (Figure 2.8).

	A	B	C	D	E	F
1	hotel	is_canceled	lead_time	arrival_date_year	arrival_date_month	arrival_date_week_numb
2	Resort Hotel	0	342	2015	July	27
3	Resort Hotel	0	737	2015	July	27
4	Resort Hotel	0	7	2015	July	27
5	Resort Hotel	0	13	2015	July	27
6	Resort Hotel	0	14	2015	July	27
7	Resort Hotel	0	14	2015	July	27
8	Resort Hotel	0	0	2015	July	27
9	Resort Hotel	0	9	2015	July	27
10	Resort Hotel	1	85	2015	July	27
11	Resort Hotel	1	75	2015	July	27
12	Resort Hotel	1	23	2015	July	27
13	Resort Hotel	0	35	2015	July	27
14	Resort Hotel	0	68	2015	July	27
15	Resort Hotel	0	18	2015	July	27
16	Resort Hotel	0	37	2015	July	27
17	Resort Hotel	0	68	2015	July	27
18	Resort Hotel	0	37	2015	July	27
19	Resort Hotel	0	12	2015	July	27
20	Resort Hotel	0	0	2015	July	27
21	Resort Hotel	0	7	2015	July	27
22	Resort Hotel	0	37	2015	July	27
23	Resort Hotel	0	72	2015	July	27

FIGURE 2.8 Hotel Dataset.

```
E: > DATA SETS > main.py > ...
import pandas as pd
from pandas_profiling import profile_report

#Loading the dataset
df = pd.read_csv("E:\DATA SETS\hotel_bookings.csv")
print(df)
#Generate a report
profile = profile_report.ProfileReport(df) #minimal == true can be used to reduce the output dat
stream
profile.to_file(output_file = "hoteling.html")

```

Dataset statistics

Number of variables	32
Number of observations	3021
Missing cells	5630
Missing cells (%)	5.8%
Duplicate rows	0
Duplicate rows (%)	0.0%

Variable types

Categorical	22
Numeric	10

FIGURE 2.9 Descriptive Statistics.

- **Step I – Descriptive statistics**

From the given dataset, descriptive statistics is carried out and its outcome is presented in Figure 2.9.

Figure 2.9 shows the details of dataset. The dataset contains raw data that contain missing values, incomplete attributes or may contain noisy and aggregate data. However, in order to make quality and accurate decisions, the data should be accurate, complete, value-added, consistent and should not contain and noisy data. Therefore, there is a need to preprocess the data as raw data cannot be read by algorithm due to errors. The data can be sorted into categories for better understanding and it is also useful for association rule mining. From the parameters and variables, we can create a scatterplot that shows correlations of various parameters. From this plot, we can see the black lines which represent invalid parameters. So to bring clarity and smooth the noisy data, we need to remove the parameters that are of no use in our analysis. Therefore, we need to remove parameters such as days in waiting list, previous booking cancellations, etc. The correlation plot is depicted in Figure 2.10.

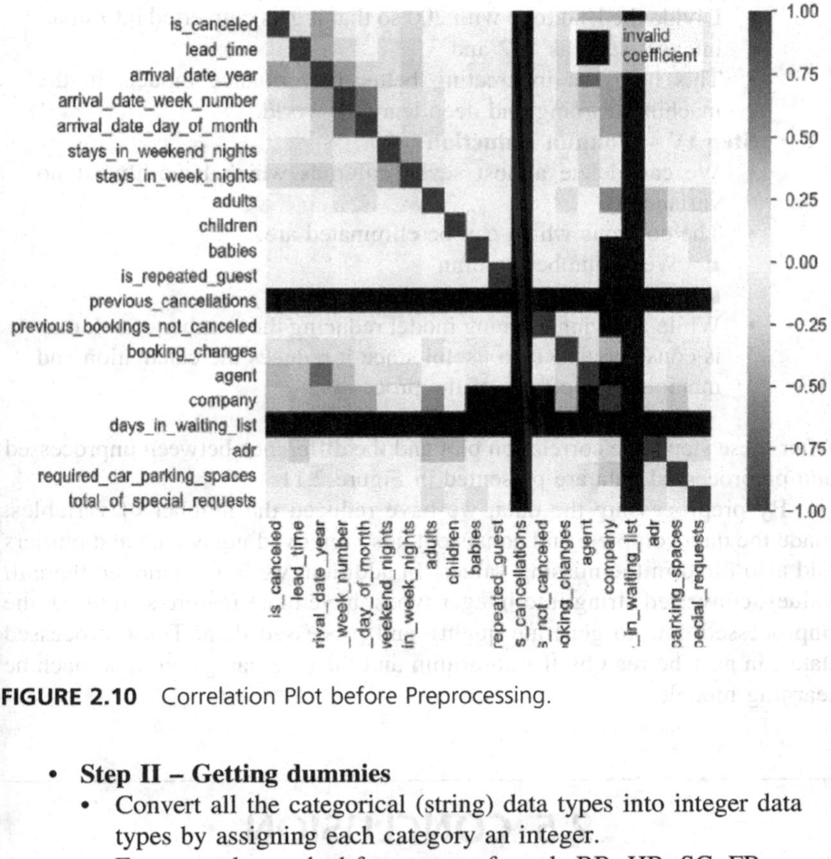

FIGURE 2.10 Correlation Plot before Preprocessing.

- **Step II – Getting dummies**
  - Convert all the categorical (string) data types into integer data types by assigning each category an integer.
  - For example, we had four types of meals BB, HB, SC, FB.
  - Convert these values into integers, such that BB == 1; HB == 2; SC == 3; FB == 4.
  - Since integer values are a lot easier to be processed rather than string values.
  - So, we can get the dummies for all the categorical values that we had.
- **Step III – Feature scaling**
  - Feature scaling is dividing a number with a suitable number such that the huge numbers maybe integers or floating points are converted into smaller and easy to calculate numbers.
  - In this case we have two real-valued columns: lead time and average daily rate (adr).

    - Divide the lead time with 200 so that it gets converted into small integers such as 1, 2 and 3.
    - This helps us in creating better performance models in the machine learning and deep learning world.
- **Step IV – Column reduction**
    - We can delete almost seven columns which have almost no variance.
    - The columns which can be eliminated are:
        - Week number column
        - Previous bookings cancellation
    - While applying learning model reducing the number of columns is considered to be a useful since it reduces the calculation and manipulation efforts of the processor.

After these steps, the correlation plot and the difference between unprocessed and preprocessed data are presented in Figure 2.11.

By preprocessing the data, we have reduced the number of variables, made the data complete and consistent, also removed noisy data and outliers and also filled in the missing values. In addition, we have removed the null values, converted string into integer types, have done feature scaling on the unprocessed data to generate quality and processed data. These processed data can now be read by the algorithm and then we can generate a machine learning model.

2.5 CONCLUSION

This chapter presents the detailed overview of data storytelling along with its importance and the major roles in the data science workflow. Important steps in the analytics are also presented and discussed in this chapter. Communicating with data is the main functional component in data science and is presented with the help of real-world use case for reader's better understanding. Various data science phases and their importance for business intelligence is also presented and discussed with the help of case studies in the scope of this chapter. The two case studies which include data storytelling and data preprocessing will surely help readers to understand the application of these concepts to other real-world use cases.

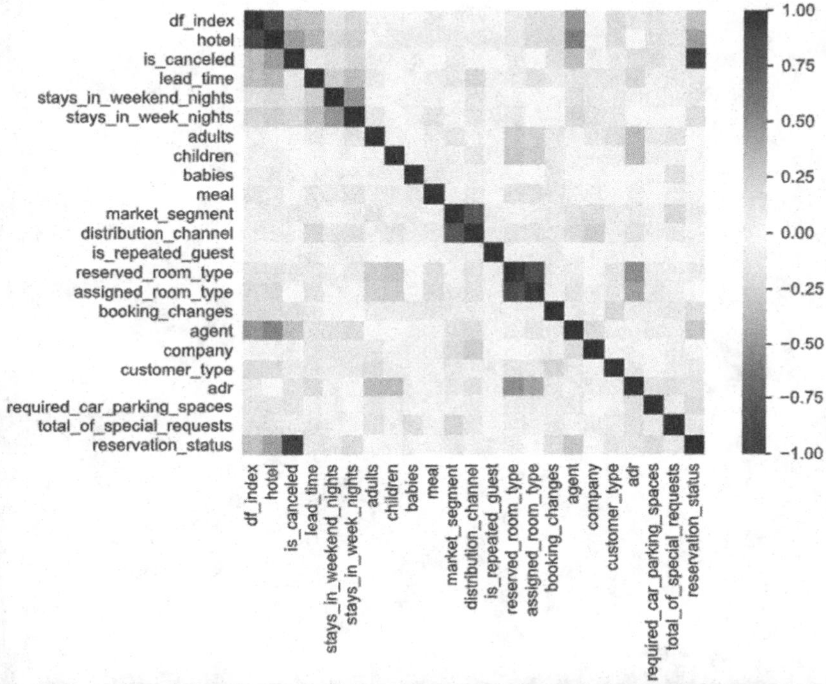

Unprocessed data		Preprocessed data	
Dataset statistics		Dataset statistics	
Number of variables	32	Number of variables	24
Number of observations	2943	Number of observations	2602
Missing cells	3134	Missing cells	0
Missing cells (%)	3.3%	Missing cells (%)	0.0%
Duplicate rows	0	Duplicate rows	0
Duplicate rows (%)	0.0%	Duplicate rows (%)	0.0%
Total size in memory	735.9 KiB	Total size in memory	488.0 KiB
Average record size in memory	256.0 B	Average record size in memory	192.0 B

FIGURE 2.11 Correlation Plot after Preprocessing.

REFERENCES

1. Allan, G., 2003. A Critique of Using Grounded Theory as a Research Method. *Electronic Journal of Business Research Methods*, 2(1), pp. 1–10.
2. Mythreyi Velmurugan, Chun Ouyang, Catarina Moreira, and Renuka Sindhgatta. Evaluating Fidelity of Explainable Methods for Predictive Process Analytics, In Proceedings of the 33rd International Conference on Advanced Information Systems Engineering (CAISE) Forum, Melbourne, Australia, 2021.

REFERENCES

Data Visualization

3

The previous chapter dealt with ways to communicate story of the data, thereby making us familiar with visualization and what needs to be conveyed. The context, the scenarios, answering the questions and then delivering the right type of visualization for the audience are the points that will now be discussed in detail in this chapter.

Let us have an understanding and make ourselves familiar with the details of viz (visualization)!!!

3.1 NEED FOR VISUALIZATION

It is believed that picture tells a thousand words. Hence, a visualization will definitely communicate the data more effectively.

A good visualization can change the entire perspective. 'It is not how much you are communicating through a visualization but how you are communicating'. Does the visualization give meaningful insights is the question that should be addressed. Therefore, we need visualization to comprehend the data, to understand it and to interpret it. On the other bright side, a data viz designer will help and assist a data scientist to recognize, identify and know more about the data as well. Still, question arises, why to visualize? Can't a text table or numbers convey the information? Let us take an example. Assume a person is owing a start-up and has a presentation with a Venture Capitalist to invest in the company. The presentation definitely should comprise details that would make the investor satisfied and make a decision to invest in the company. A text table with lot of figures about projects undertaken, turnover and so on will make it difficult for him to convince the audience and to convey the important milestones. A story needs to be communicated effectively through the data by understanding the requirements of audience [1].

DOI: 10.1201/9781003307747-3

Role	Q1	Q2	Q3
Regional Manager	1.5 million	1 million	2 million
Account manager	0.5 million	0.3 million	0.8 million

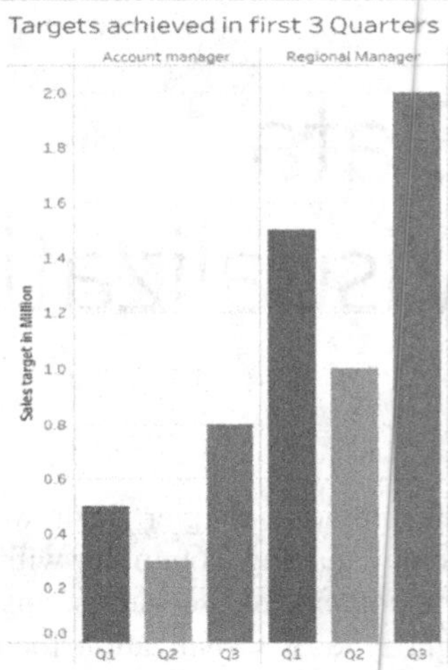

FIGURE 3.1 A Text Table and a Bar Graph.

A visualization will assist here in getting the ball rolling!!!

Consider one more scenario where the data about sales targets need to be presented to higher-level management, for example a simple bar graph will help in understanding the data better rather than text table is presented in Figure 3.1. (A hypothetical data about sales targets by individuals is presented in the figures.)

A visualization is not just a picture or a collage that is depicted beautifully. It is something more. A visualization can be a chart, an image, a simple video or even a dashboard. A representation that depicts the data contents.

Necessity of visualization arises where – from business impacts – some crucial information needs to be understood. It showcases the analytics, the relationships of data points, some insights that are made clear and understandable. Viz explains the trends, the patterns, the forecast – one can have good explanatory analysis through them.

For every business, leveraging meaningful data is crucial part. Data visualization thus reveals these insights.

3.2 COMMUNICATING VISUALLY

While we have now understood about fundamentals about visualization, there is a dire need to have effective communication through visualization. While communicating, it is necessary to understand and know the audience and their requirements [2].

Communication visually implies that we are trying to reduce the burden of going through the textual contents by presenting the data in a pictorial form. Word of caution – visualization is not making things look nice, it is communication which leads to interpretations by the audience. Always remember the following while making a viz:

- Who is the audience?
- What questions are been addressed through the visualization?
- Does the visualization satisfy the demands and needs of them?

Assume a CFO of a company wants to seek information with regard to the sales, profits achieved in quarters. Moreover information about the best performer and best-seller product is also to be identified along with the trends in the patterns. A data with numbers do not suffice the needs nor will it be effective but this communication through visuals can reveal and showcase the data and analytics in an effective way.

Communicating visually essentially means to have effective a pictorial display. But this display should be such that the audience is attracted toward it. The visualization must meet the demands where the need of further explanation is minimal and the viz communicates everything with accuracy.

As a data viz designer, ensure that, while communicating visually one should:

- Have knowledge about target audience
- Understand needs of the audience
- Apply cognitive principles
- Keep the viz simple

Putting them to practice, will help to bring out a creative, attentive visualization. It is said that the viz should convey the story of the data. Let us narrow down to the points.

3.2.1 About the Audience

To communicate given data, different ways of visualization are possible, but the one that captures audience attention is desired. Further, to communicate the same data, the perspective, the context of the audience, is going to impact the nature in which the viz needs to be created and designed. It is always preferred prior to creation of the viz, that 'personas' of the audience should be studied. Persona can be thought of a very short brief of the audience. This helps the designer to know more about the goals, the requirements and knowledge of the audience.

A sample persona is shown with few parameters as mentioned. This enables to make the visualizations to be generated in line with the skill set of the audience.

Further, the level of detailing that the visualization should present should be accounted. In this aspect, the knowledge or familiarity of the audience can act as a barrier in the process. So, the persona assists to a great extent here. They are helpful in determining the extent to which audience can be given control for the visualizations. And most important – as a data viz designer, ensure that the needs of the target audience are met.

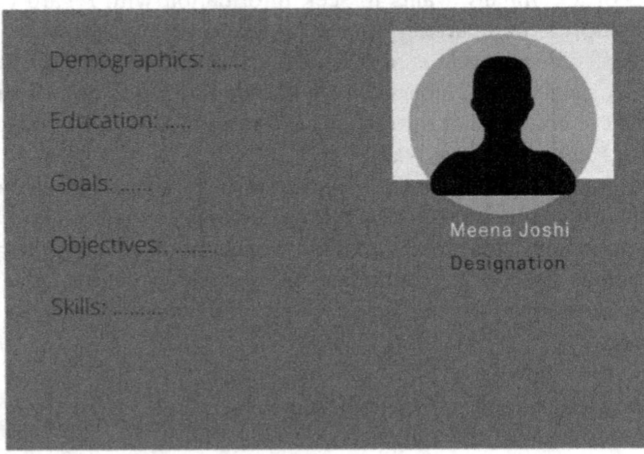

A sample format of persona.

In the view of cognitive principles, realizing the need to reduce the cognitive load and at the same time making the viz less cluttered is expected. The amount of mental effort should be minimal in the view of interpretation of the created viz. Making a fancy viz is not what you communicate from the data, but perhaps a simple one is preferred, thereby giving good and accurate insights. Though a debatable question, 'keep it simple' is the rule!!! (A simple bar chart can be more effective that a fancy visualization.) The viz should hit the iconic memory of the audience, thereby making an impact.

3.2.1.1 Tools to Communicate Visually

Currently, lot of tools are available at present to create viz, thereby opening a new era of opportunities in visualization community. Power BI, Tableau,

Datawrapper, knime are the ones used. Though as a data scientist, python or for that matter even R can be used in visualization, these tools possess tremendous potential to unleash the data and create 'content-rich' visualizations.

We will explore more in Tableau in next chapter with viz creation.

3.3 VISUALIZATION MYTHS AND REALITY

As we deep dive in this world of viz, and the more we create it, we realize that it's not a cake walk nor is a fancy way to create it!!! Lot of myths revolve around this, and as a designer it is necessary to know that viz designing and creation is not an easy task!!!

3.3.1 Creating Viz Is Very Easy

One would get fascinated looking at an opportunity to work as a data viz designer. The job though is not an easy one. Just as a data scientist is responsible to have a hold on the algorithms and perform analytics, the viz designer is responsible to showcase the insight, make use of analytics to convey the desired information. It is a process where data are being translated into a visual pattern.

Creation of viz is not a click of a button to generate the chart. It requires lot of skills, effort and thought process that conveys about the data in the from of viz. It is an iterative process where different variants of same data can be generated and misleading information can be eliminated by the designer.

So, the task needs skills, understanding and lot of patience to come up with good viz!

3.3.2 Viz Is All about Making Data Look Fancy Pictorially

In any visualization, aesthetics plays an important role, but it is not just for making the visualization pretty. The color combinations used, the contrast, the range of hues, color palette type and moreover making the visualization accessible to all is expected.

This is critical where one would use Gestalt's principles which talk about the ways in which good effective visualizations can be created and the pre-attentive attributes of color or shape need knowledge and familiarity about their usage and in which scenarios they are applicable. A wow factor is not possible without proper understanding of the data and these principles.

Therefore, creating visualization is not at all having a scenic picture being displayed.

As an example, a visualization is shown in Figure 3.2(b). It is generated from electronic store dataset. A snapshot of the dataset is shown as well in Figure 3.2(a). The dataset is about the electronic products sales along with their profits, discounts, customer details and so on.

From the visualization shown, important noteworthy factors are been communicated. First, it is not a simple bar graph that is shown, instead it depicts the products which despite having good sales revenue generated, resulted in loss. The colors used capture the attention of audience thereby highlighting the ones in maroon color. Such a visualization definitely gives more insights for decision making from the product sales planning.

(a)

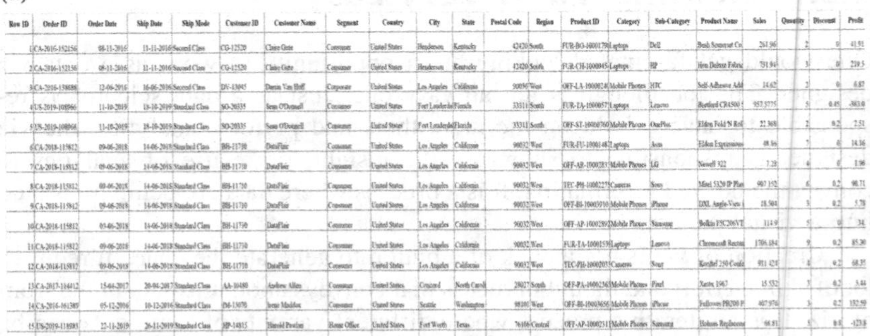

Row ID	Order ID	Order Date	Ship Date	Ship Mode	Customer ID	Customer Name	Segment	Country	City	State	Postal Code	Region	Product ID	Category	Sub-Category	Product Name	Sales	Quantity	Discount	Profit
1	CA-2016-152156	08-11-2016	11-11-2016	Second Class	CG-12520	Claire Gute	Consumer	United States	Henderson	Kentucky	42420	South	FUR-BO-10001798	Laptops	Dell	Bush Somerset Co	261.96	2	0	41.91
2	CA-2016-152156	08-11-2016	11-11-2016	Second Class	CG-12520	Claire Gute	Consumer	United States	Henderson	Kentucky	42420	South	FUR-CH-10000454	Laptops	HP	Hon Deluxe Fabric	731.94	3	0	219.5
3	CA-2016-138688	12-06-2016	16-06-2016	Second Class	DV-13045	Darrin Van Huff	Corporate	United States	Los Angeles	California	90036	West	OFF-LA-10000240	Mobile Phones	HTC	Self-Adhesive Add	14.62	2	0	6.87
4	US-2019-108966	11-10-2019	18-10-2019	Standard Class	SO-20335	Sean O'Donnell	Consumer	United States	Fort Lauderdale	Florida	33311	South	FUR-TA-10000577	Laptops	Lenovo	Bretford CR4500 S	957.5775	5	0.45	-383.0
5	US-2019-108966	11-10-2019	18-10-2019	Standard Class	SO-20335	Sean O'Donnell	Consumer	United States	Fort Lauderdale	Florida	33311	South	OFF-ST-10000760	Mobile Phones	OnePlus	Eldon Fold 'N Rol	22.368	2	0.2	2.51
6	CA-2018-115812	09-06-2018	14-06-2018	Standard Class	BH-11710	DataFlair	Consumer	United States	Los Angeles	California	90032	West	FUR-FU-10001487	Laptops	Asus	Eldon Expressions	48.86	7	0	14.16
7	CA-2018-115812	09-06-2018	14-06-2018	Standard Class	BH-11710	DataFlair	Consumer	United States	Los Angeles	California	90032	West	OFF-AR-10002833	Mobile Phones	LG	Newell 322	7.28	4	0	1.96
8	CA-2018-115812	09-06-2018	14-06-2018	Standard Class	BH-11710	DataFlair	Consumer	United States	Los Angeles	California	90032	West	TEC-PH-10002275	Cameras	Sony	Mitel 5320 IP Pho	907.152	6	0.2	90.71
9	CA-2018-115812	09-06-2018	14-06-2018	Standard Class	BH-11710	DataFlair	Consumer	United States	Los Angeles	California	90032	West	OFF-BI-10003910	Mobile Phones	iPhone	DXL Angle-View	18.504	3	0.2	5.78
10	CA-2018-115812	09-06-2018	14-06-2018	Standard Class	BH-11710	DataFlair	Consumer	United States	Los Angeles	California	90032	West	OFF-AP-10002892	Mobile Phones	Samsung	Belkin F5C206VT	114.9	5	0	34
11	CA-2018-115812	09-06-2018	14-06-2018	Standard Class	BH-11710	DataFlair	Consumer	United States	Los Angeles	California	90032	West	FUR-TA-10001539	Laptops	Lenovo	Chromcraft Rectan	1706.184	9	0.2	85.30
12	CA-2018-115812	09-06-2018	14-06-2018	Standard Class	BH-11710	DataFlair	Consumer	United States	Los Angeles	California	90032	West	TEC-PH-10002033	Cameras	Sony	Konftel 250 Confe	911.424	4	0.2	68.35
13	CA-2017-114412	15-04-2017	20-04-2017	Standard Class	AA-10480	Andrew Allen	Consumer	United States	Concord	North Caroli	28027	South	OFF-PA-10002365	Mobile Phones	Pixel	Xerox 1967	15.552	3	0.2	5.44
14	CA-2016-161389	05-12-2016	10-12-2016	Standard Class	IM-15070	Irene Maddox	Consumer	United States	Seattle	Washington	98103	West	OFF-BI-10003656	Mobile Phones	iPhone	Fellowes PB200 P	407.976	3	0.2	132.59
15	US-2019-118983	22-11-2019	26-11-2019	Standard Class	HP-14815	Harold Pawlan	Home Office	United States	Fort Worth	Texas	76106	Central	OFF-AP-10002311	Mobile Phones	Samsung	Holmes Replaceme	68.81	5	0.8	-123.8
16	US-2019-118983	22-11-2019	26-11-2019	Standard Class	HP-14815	Harold Pawlan	Home Office	United States	Fort Worth	Texas	76106	Central	OFF-BI-10000756	Mobile Phones	iPhone	Storex DuraTech R	2.544	3	0.8	-3.8
17	CA-2018-105893	11-11-2018	18-11-2018	Standard Class	PK-19075	Pete Kriz	Consumer	United States	Madison	Wisconsin	53711	Central	OFF-ST-10004186	Mobile Phones	OnePlus	Stur-D-Stor Shelvi	665.88	6	0	13.31
18	CA-2018-167164	13-05-2018	15-05-2018	Second Class	AG-10270	Alejandro Grove	Consumer	United States	West Jordan	Utah	84084	West	OFF-ST-10000107	Mobile Phones	OnePlus	Fellowes Super St	55.5	2	0	9

(b)

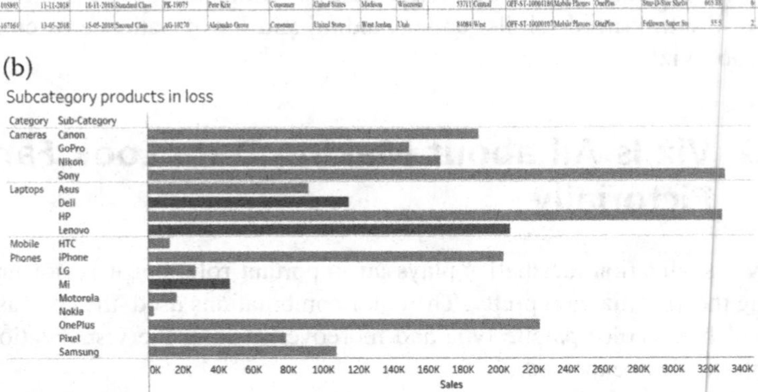

FIGURE 3.2 (a) Sample Dataset, (b) Subcategory Products Resulting in Loss.

3.3.3 Creation of Viz Is an Elaborate and Expensive Process

It is believed that visualization creation is a very elaborative, tiresome and expensive process. The process of visualization creation is in fact a thoughtful one. To create data visualization, availability of interactive tools with powerful capabilities to showcase the data and its patterns is now in reach. The mechanism in which the visualization is accessible is important here.

A viz can be generated on a paper or by use of the tools; it is about effective communication of the data. Definitely not an elaborative process, yet requires skills to portray the data.

3.4 ETHICS IN VISUALIZATION

'Ethics in visualization?' sounds weird!!! As human beings we have our own ethics which we tend to follow, similarly, some principles are to be followed in visualization too. The main reason to employ these ethics is to avoid miscommunication and misinterpretation of the viz. The visualization created must convey the crux and at the same time be accurate and not misleading. Imagine a scenario where one is presented with a visualization and, sadly, the interpretation is misleading. This can be a grave issue in case of sensitive data especially in medical domain. An example of this is discussed next.

Consider dataset in Table 3.1. The dataset comprises particular virus cases and deaths in a region. For a government official, a visualization is to be created to show the status for the said period about cases reported so that further actions can be planned. A line chart, a pattern of cases reported is shown in Figures 3.3(a) and 3.3(b).

From the visualization in Figure 3.3(a), one can immediately infer looking at the line chart that the cases are decreasing. On contrary, the x-axis is reversed, misleading information is been communicated. The years in which the data are presented on the axis are incorrect. Same way in Figure 3.3(b) the inverted y-axis is again giving a wrong perspective of the cases, and hence these practices should be avoided in designing the visualizations. Thus, a wrong scenario is presented.

One more ethic that needs to be applied and followed in data visualization is of bar chart start axis. Whenever the visuals are shown we try to compare the endpoints. In case of bar charts, if the axis does not start at zero, the interpretation of the data shown is wrong. Figure 3.4 shows a bar chart

TABLE 3.1 Dataset of Virus Outbreak in a Region

MONTH	*CASES REPORTED*	*DEATHS*
Jan-20	0	0
Feb-20	0	0
Mar-20	0	0
Apr-20	10	1
May-20	14	2
Jun-20	19	4
Jul-20	200	5
Aug-20	250	4
Sep-20	130	4
Oct-20	170	7
Nov-20	155	3
Dec-20	278	8
Jan-21	344	14
Feb-21	175	9
Mar-21	248	11
Apr-21	109	12
May-21	96	3
Jun-21	87	5
Jul-21	100	3

with percentage of people vaccinated in a specific area. As mentioned earlier, we compare endpoints. The figure mentioned wrong, shows vast difference between the percentages of October and November month as the y-axis does not start at 0, whereas in case of second bar chart, it is accurately mentioned.

Pie chart is one of the visualizations that is commonly used and preferred by many of us. In data visualization, a notion of 'pie chart controversy' exists. There is a need of clarity whether to use and when to use the pie chart. One should make a note that it is fine to use a pie chart when there are few points of comparison, especially three to four. Most importantly, it is best to use when the proportions of the data compared are significantly different and varied.

Figure 3.5 depicts wrong and right ways for the pie chart. Figure on the right is a proper and appropriate way for the pie-chart usage. The pie chart is about percentage of people who like which fruits. From the figure on the left, excluding the proportion of bananas, the remaining fruits are seen with same size of the area coverage. Hence, from the proportion area shown in the pie chart, one cannot make it the percentages. Thus, explicitly labelling is made

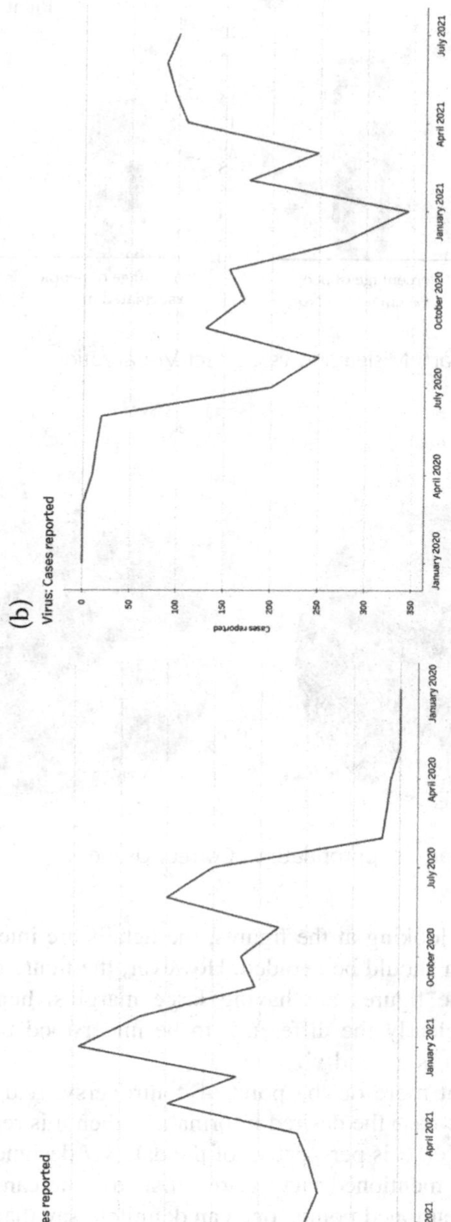

FIGURE 3.3 (a) Normal Scenario (b) Inverted *y*-axis. Pattern of Virus Cases Reported in a Region.

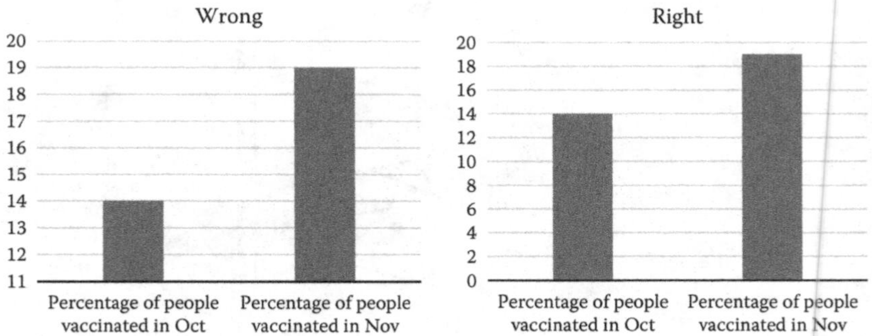

FIGURE 3.4 Bar Chart: Misleading vs Correct Visualization.

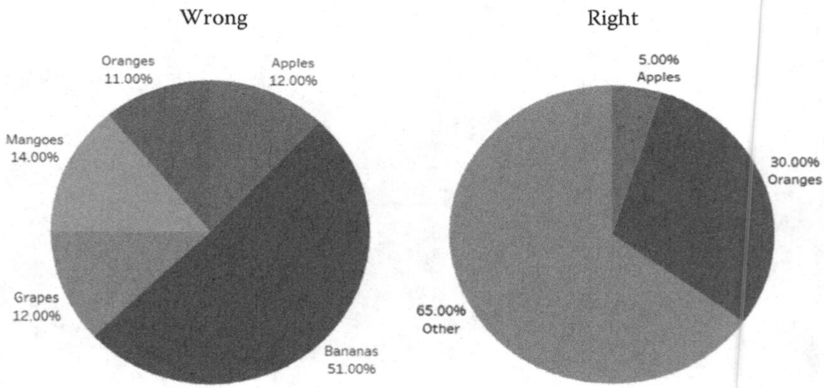

FIGURE 3.5 Pie Chart: Inappropriate vs Correct Usage.

and then only after looking at the figures, the details are interpreted. Such a type of visualization should be avoided. However, the figure on the right, the pie chart shows the figures are having large margins, hence the area of coverage conveys clearly the difference to be understood by the audience. Such a visualization is a good viz.

Let us highlight more on the point of controversy. If using a bar chart simply one can showcase the desired information, then it is recommended not to use a pie chart. Yet, it is perspective of the data viz designer if he wants to use it (ensuring the mentioned factors are satisfied), one can go for it.

From above-mentioned points, one can definitely say that there are lot of best practices to be employed in the visualization creation. Few other points that should be considered in the viz creation process are as follows:

- Use of proper contrast
- Addition of heading, caption
- Use of correct color, shape and size
- Avoiding overuse or underuse of color
- Avoiding putting too many things on the viz
- Never convey misleading visuals

Always in visualization, the colors definitely are an important factor that captures audience attention. Along with that the heading, labelling of the data points, annotations as required should be added in the charts. In viz creation, it is said that do not overuse or underuse the colors. Appropriate contrast colors and levels of brightness should be used to make the viz catchy. Effective usage of shapes and the size of shapes too convey significant information.

Many times, the intent behind the visualization is not wrong but the visual arguments are proposing inappropriate and misleading information. These cases should be taken care of and as a data viz designer, it is our job to give 'accurate insights'.

3.5 RIGHT GRAPH FOR RIGHT DATA

Coming to a fundamental question – what type of chart/graph is best for my visualization? Indeed, a confusing question and one might ponder on the different available options to show and communicate the insights.

After having detailed discussion on the ethics, the need for communicating visually, let us try to understand that under which scenarios or circumstances which type of visualization is best suited. Necessarily, the type and nature of the data [3] to be conveyed is going to determine the visualization type that would be used. From the list of options available, we will go into highlighting the type and when to use it along with the data.

1. Simple text tables: A text table is a part of visualization but is used and should be used only when the numbers to be communicated are very few. By few we mean to say that it is just two to four numbers of comparisons that need to be shown; thus, a simple text table can be preferred here. Though not recommended, they can be used depending on your target audience perspective.

   A sample text table is shown in Table 3.2 that displays the count of students familiar with different languages.

TABLE 3.2 Text Table

PYTHON	*R*	*JAVA*
1255	547	298

2. Bar chart: A most common preferred option and a favorite one of data viz designers.

   A bar chart would be used to depict the comparisons and rankings. Compositions of the parameters can be well conveyed through a stacked bar chart. It is necessary to determine and identify the parameters, the labelling and type of bar chart to be used with reference to the data points. A stacked bar chart is depicted in Figure 3.6(a) that displays proportion of sales in each category. Dataset used is mentioned in Figure 3.2(a).
3. Line chart: While dealing with the trends, to observe pattern, a line chart is preferred. One can definitely say that to observe changes over a period of time, line chart becomes a good option to use. In line chart, spark charts too can be used to determine the quick trends – typically used in stock markets. Data to go for temporal relationship will be best suited with line chart.
4. Scatter plots: A type of visualization used to understand the co-relationship between data points. Often this type of visualization will be used to determine the impact/effect of one parameter to other. It is a type of chart to show relationship between variables of a dataset. For example, relationship between the age and salary.
5. Histograms and box plots: To understand the distributions of the data, the nature histograms and boxplots are used. These charts give deep insights about the data thereby helping from analytics side as well. Box plots assist with the quartiles, means and outliers giving us more knowledge about the data. Thus, a continuous data type to see its distributions, frequencies will be employed here.
6. Highlight tables and heat maps: Highlight tables use colors for comparison. Heat maps are used when one has to visualize lot of data at a glance and at the same time, the hot spots are also to be identified. Heat maps use sizes and color to show the comparisons between the categories and parameters.
7. Tree maps: To exploit hierarchical relationships, a tree map is recommended. Tree maps open a broader view to narrow down into the hierarchical details. A very nice and an effective chart type that explains the part to whole relationship. A sunburst chart is also used to show hierarchical representation.

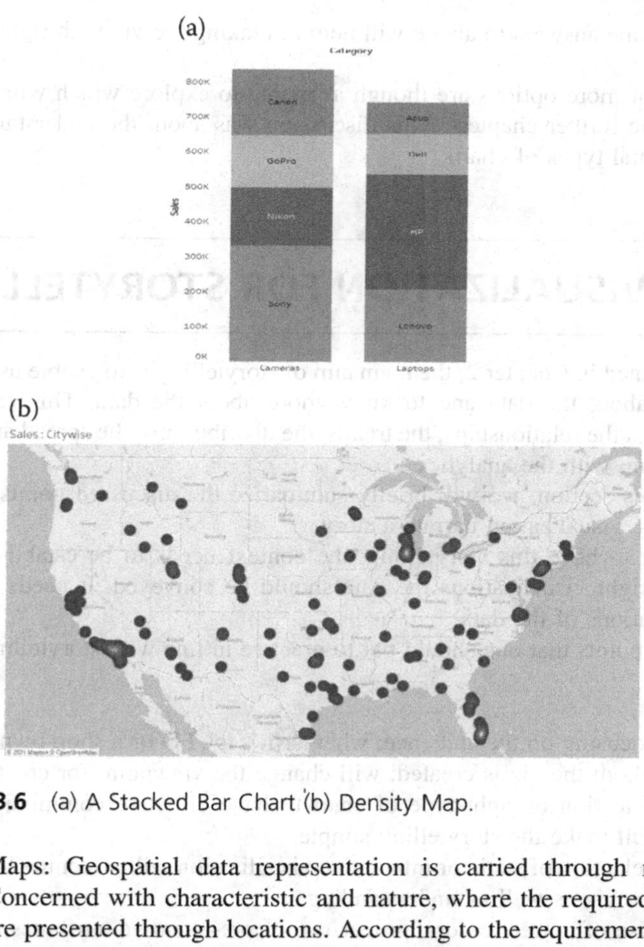

FIGURE 3.6 (a) A Stacked Bar Chart (b) Density Map.

8. Maps: Geospatial data representation is carried through maps. Concerned with characteristic and nature, where the required data are presented through locations. According to the requirement one can go in creation of maps, for example, density maps.

   A sample density map is shown in Figure 3.6(b) using the dataset mentioned in Figure 3.2(a).

   The viz describes the sales generated with respect to regions.

Based on the fundamental types of charts mentioned, one must think of following before selecting any of the charts:

1. What type of data are to be used?
2. Is there any relationship that needs to be identified among the data parameters?
3. What does the audience want?

Knowing the answers to above will help in making the viz with right type of charts.

Lot of more options are though available to explore which will be covered in the further chapters. This discussion was about the understanding of fundamental types of charts.

3.6 VISUALIZATION FOR STORYTELLING

As explained in Chapter 2, the main aim of storytelling is to enable user to get insights about the data and to know more about the data. This can be to understand the relationships, the trends, the distributions, the spread and much more along with the analytics.

In this section, we will briefly summarize the discussed points thereby letting the visualization narrate a story.

Now to have this storytelling, the context needs to be established and through right visualizations the data should be conveyed. It needs accurate interpretations of the data.

The points that one should put to practice in line with storytelling are as follows:

1. Focusing on the audience: whether it's a CFO or a shop owner for whom the viz is created; will change the viewpoint for creation.
2. Selection of right type of chart to have effective communication will make the storytelling simple.
3. Selection of static or interactive visualization will affect the look of the viz as well as understanding.
4. Use of correct colors, proper use of pre-attentive attributes, reducing the clutter will result in building a good viz.
5. The level of detailing, highlighting, labelling adds more to make the viz better.
6. Hitting the iconic memory of the end user makes things simple as a viz designer to explain.
7. Adding annotations, analytics as desired to convey the story will drive the storytelling in a very effective and acceptable way from the audience perspective.
8. Finally, bringing it together on a dashboard, linking the charts to tell the story, results in having a wonderful and meaningful viz!!!

To conclude, use of visualization to tell a story is far more effective and appropriate means thereby enabling the end user gaining potential vision, understanding and forecast about the data!!! Chapter 4 discusses this storytelling in the form of a case study.

3.7 CONCLUSION

The chapter discusses the necessity and effectiveness to communicate data through visualizations. Unleashing the potential to build powerful visualizations and thereby making readers familiar with the primitives of visualization is discussed in this chapter. Overcoming the myths and building effective yet simple visualizations to dive in the world of data viz is discussed. Factors of appropriate chart selection to ethics to be followed are also addressed. Further chapter opens a new dimension of viz through Tableau for budding viz designer!

REFERENCES

1. 'Storytelling with data, lets practice', C N Knaflic, Wiley.
2. https://www.infocepts.com/pdf/books/InfoCepts_Data_Storytelling_Book.pdf
3. Liu, J., Tang, T., Wang, W. D., Xu, B., Kong, X. and Xia, F., 2018. A Survey of Scholarly Data Visualization. *IEEE Access*, 6, pp. 19205–19221.

Visualization with Tableau

4

4.1 OVERVIEW

Tableau [1] enables us to come up with a wide range of visualizations to address the needs of the target audience. It is all about delivering good visualizations. From the audience perspective, the audience persona is very important. As, we are addressing questions of the audience, keeping in mind the pointers discussed in Chapter 3 one has to generate and build the visualizations. Knowing the type of data, the aesthetics, effective medium and channel [2] are crucial factors to having eye-catching visualizations.

4.1.1 About Tableau

A data visualization is a tool that helps us to connect to different data sources and generate visualizations. Csv, Json, spatial, text and many more formats are supported, and with Tableau one can design and develop viz with interactive user interface. Tableau is a smart tool that can in fact recommend which type of viz or chart is best suited for the dataset with the purpose being served.

4.1.2 Using Tableau

Tableau deployment comes in different types depending on the functionalities required. The discussion in the book will be based on Tableau Public, a free platform made available to create and share the viz publicly. So, simply put your mail id and install it. Once installed and opened for the first time, Start page – screen of Tableau public will be seen as shown

DOI: 10.1201/9781003307747-4

in Figure 4.1(a). With reference to the Figure 4.1(a), the options of Connect, Open and Discover are seen. Connect, as is visible, helps us connect to the type of file to create viz. Under the open option, on the right side, 'Open from Tableau public' is available. This is for opening the file that has been already saved to Tableau Public. Once we start creating visualizations, the ones saved on Tableau will be seen under this option at the same time, they would be visible in empty area below open. Discover is provided to inspire Tableau users with the latest visualizations, getting to know about the visualization community, to see effective visualizations and at the same time, there are lot of videos and posts that can assist the user. It shows viz of the day too!! One point to mention here is that visualization communities are very much active on social media and one should definitely follow to know more about the recent ways and means to create an effective viz [3].

4.1.3 About Workbook

While working with Tableau Public, one can create multiple visualizations under one workbook and they are saved in form of .tbw. The contents are published on Tableau once saved and one can share the link of his/her visualizations.

4.2 FUNCTIONAL COMPONENTS

The section will discuss about the different components of Tableau. Most of them will be used during the visualization creation and are of immense importance. Figure 4.1(b) shows the use of extreme left button that acts as toggle to shift between two screens – Start page to Data page. On clicking it, the Data page shown in Figure 4.1(c) is visible. This is necessary to understand that one can use the toggle button and have the desired dataset connected.

Let us first connect to a sample dataset to enable us understand the functionalities. From Figure 4.1(b) or (c), select 'connect to data'. Tableau provides various formats for this connection. In this case here, we will be connecting to an excel file. Table 4.1 shows the dataset for sales in a medical store for reference.

Figure 4.2(a) shows the screen after connection to the medical store dataset mentioned in Table 4.1. Select sheet1 from the bottom pane of Figure 4.2(a), screen in Figure 4.2(b) is visible. Now we are ready to go. As the dataset has just one excel sheet, the same is visible in Figure 4.2(a). If there were multiple

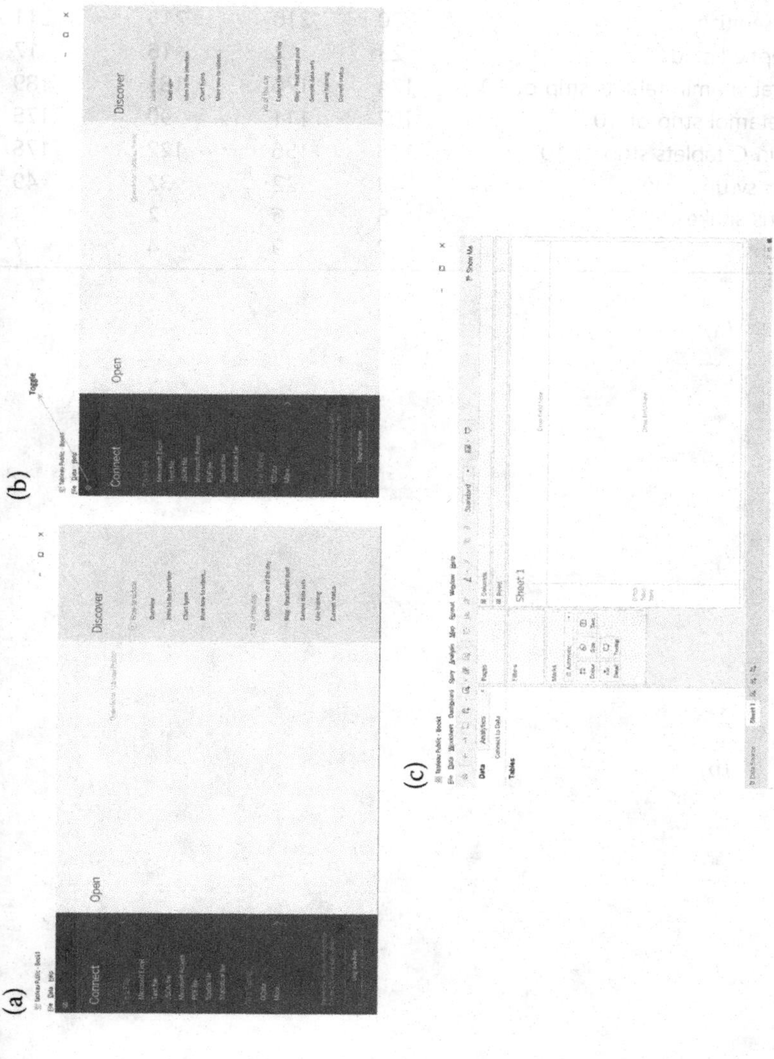

FIGURE 4.1 (a) Start Page – Screen after Installation of Tableau Public (b) Use of Toggle from Start Page (c) After Toggle – Data Page.

TABLE 4.1 Sample Dataset – Medical Store

ITEMS	*JAN*	*FEB*	*MARCH*	*APRIL*
Surgical masks	675	800	478	700
N95 masks	403	566	786	932
Hand sanitizers	320	210	215	211
Antiseptic liquids	23	12	16	17
General vitamin tablets strip of 10	124	176	184	189
Paracetamol strip of 10	102	111	90	175
Vitamin C tablets strip of 10	143	156	122	178
Cough syrup	43	22	32	49
Proteins shakes	5	6	2	3
Eardrops	7	9	4	7

(a)

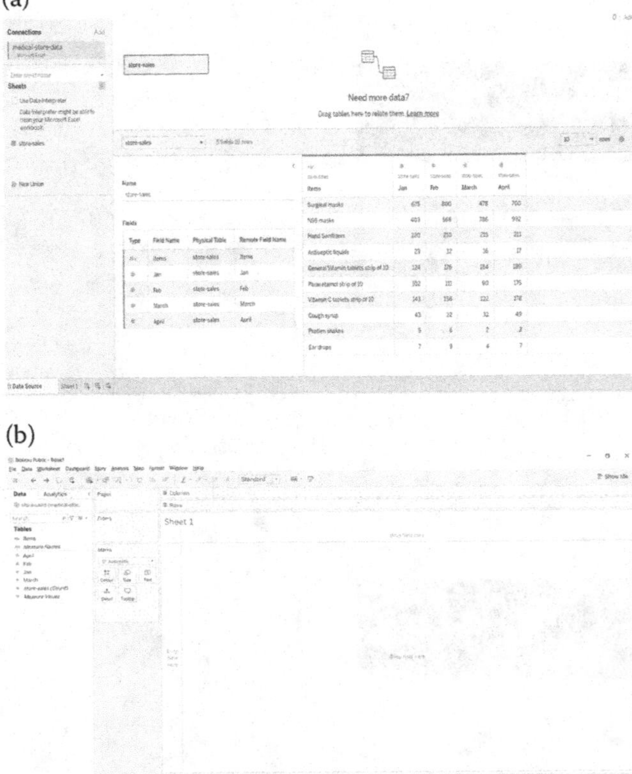

FIGURE 4.2 (a) Connected to Dataset – Medical Store Data (b) Sheet1 Post Connection to the Dataset.

sheets, then one would have to drag and drop the required one or set up association as desired. Right now, the focus will be getting basic visualizations with the single excel and understanding the parameters.

4.2.1 Measures and Dimensions

In Tableau, the data fields have different roles – dimension or measure. Each of the field that exists in the connected dataset falls under these categories. With reference to Figure 4.2(b), the left-side tables show dimensions and measures. A zoom-in view is shown in Figure 4.3(a).

From the Tables, (left corner) different parameters are available. Every field in the dataset is mapped to a data type and is assigned a role – dimension or a measure.

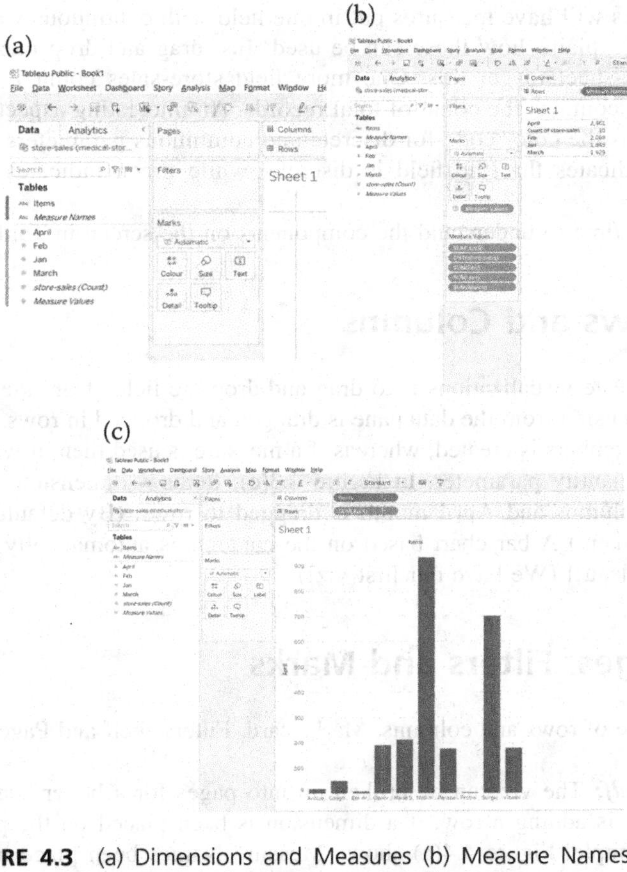

FIGURE 4.3 (a) Dimensions and Measures (b) Measure Names and Measure Values (c) Use of Rows and Columns – a Bar Chart.

The first two are (explicitly marked in blue) Items and Measure names, which are in one group. These are dimensions. Dimension in Tableau is a qualitative value. It can be a string – names, dates or even geographic data. Dimensions are used in visualization to add detailing to the view. One can get the clarity that Items is a type of string and hence it comes under dimension. Measure names is a field created by Tableau which consists of all the parameter names in the measures (discussed in the next section). Measures (explicitly marked in green) are the ones which are numeric or quantitative values. These parameters in the example are April, May, Jan which contain the count/numeric value corresponding to each of the Items. Aggregation is performed on the Measures by default in Tableau.

Two fields as discussed before which are not part of the dataset are Measure Values and Measure Names. As mentioned before Measure names will have simply all the names put in one field with discrete values and measure values will have measures put in one field with continuous values. Figure 4.3(b) explains how these can be used. Just drag and drop measure names on the sheet to get this. One more field store-sales count is also created which contains the count of total records. An interesting aspect that is noted here is the color code for discrete and continuous parameters. The blue color indicates that the field is discrete, while green indicates it is continuous.

Now it is time to understand the components on the screen in Tableau.

4.2.2 Rows and Columns

The way to create visualizations is to drag and drop the fields from the data pane. If a dimension from the data pane is dragged and dropped in rows, then a header for members is created, whereas if a measure is used then, it will be treated as a quantity parameter. In Figure 4.3(c), Items – dimension – are dragged to Columns and April month is dragged to rows. (By default, aggregation is taken.) A bar chart based on the contents is automatically generated by Tableau!! (We have our first viz!)

4.2.3 Pages, Filters and Marks

To the left side of rows and columns, Marks card, Filters shelf and Pages are visible.

Pages shelf: The viz can be broken up into pages for a better analysis perspective. It is adding a row, if a dimension is been placed on the pages shelf. For example, Figure 4.4(a) shows Measure Names been place in the

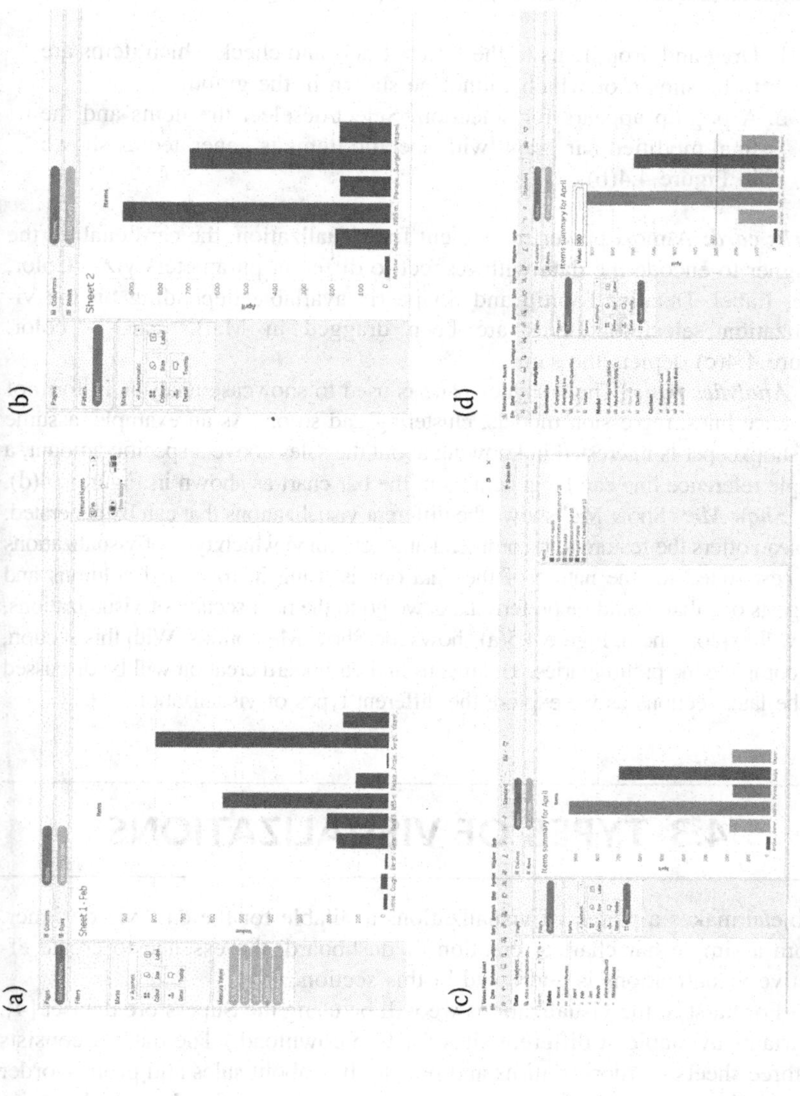

FIGURE 4.4 (a) Measure Names Placed in Pages Shelf (b) Bar Chart after Filtering Items (c) Items in Marks Card – Color (d) Use of Constant Line.

pages shelf. At the right top corner, one can have selection for month from the measure names, thus giving a viz month-wise analysis.

Filters shelf: Allows the parameters to be filtered. One can include or exclude them. For example, from a bar chart with Items and Months been dropped in columns and rows, respectively, let us apply filtering to the items selected.

1. Drag and drop items to the Filters Shelf and check which items are to be shown or which cannot be shown in the graph.
2. A pop-up appears for selection. Select/deselect the items and the final modified bar graph with specific items is generated as shown in Figure 4.4(b).

Marks card: A most powerful element for visualization, the card enables the designer to encode the data with respect to different parameters viz – Color, Size, Label, Details, Tooltip and Shape (is available depending on the visualization selected). Items are been dragged in Marks card – color. Figure 4.4(c) depicts the same.

Analytics pane: The analytics pane is used to showcase analysis in form of reference lines, regression models, clustering and so on. As an example, assume the shopkeeper is interested in knowing about the sales above a specific amount, a simple reference line can be generated in the bar chart as shown in Figure 4.4(d).

Show Me: 'Show Me' shows the different visualizations that can be generated. Tableau offers the feature to recommend and determine which type of visualizations are best suited for the nature of the data one is using in rows and columns and suggests one that would be preferred. As we go to the next section of visualizations, we will explore them. Figure 4.5(a) shows the Show Me options. With this section, we complete the preliminaries. The menus and dashboard creation will be discussed in the later sections as we explore the different types of visualizations.

4.3 TYPES OF VISUALIZATIONS

Tableau makes a platter of visualizations available for the data viz designer. From a simple bar chart to creation of dashboard, the essence to create effective visualizations is addressed in this section.

For most of the visualizations we will be using the Superstore dataset [4]. (Variants available at different sites for free download.) The dataset consists of three sheets – orders, returns and people. It is about sales and profit – order details about customers at a superstore. A snapshot of orders is shown in Figures 4.5(b) and 4.5(c).

(a)

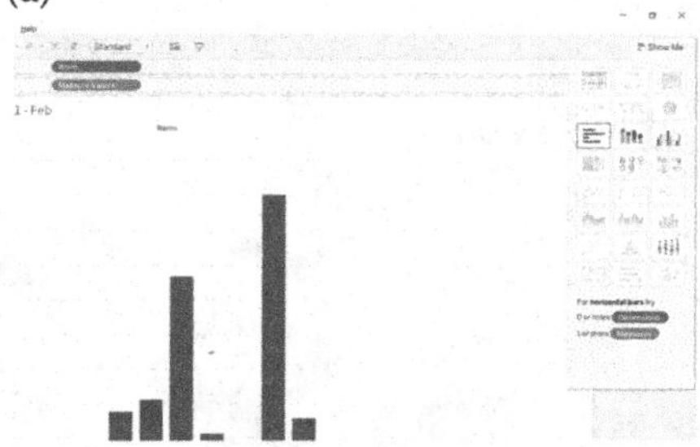

(b)

(c)

FIGURE 4.5 (a) Show Me Options (b) Superstore Dataset – Orders – Snapshot (c) Snapshot After Connecting to the Dataset and Dragging Orders.

4.3.1 Bar Chart

Though a most simple and common visualization, data viz designers tend to use this at large. The sole reason being the simplicity. The principle to 'keep is simple' in generating a viz is addressed by this and hence instead of opting for extraordinary, out-of-box visualizations which would be complex to understand, bar chart is preferred.

Basic bar chart to show Sales with respect to Category is shown in Figure 4.6(a).

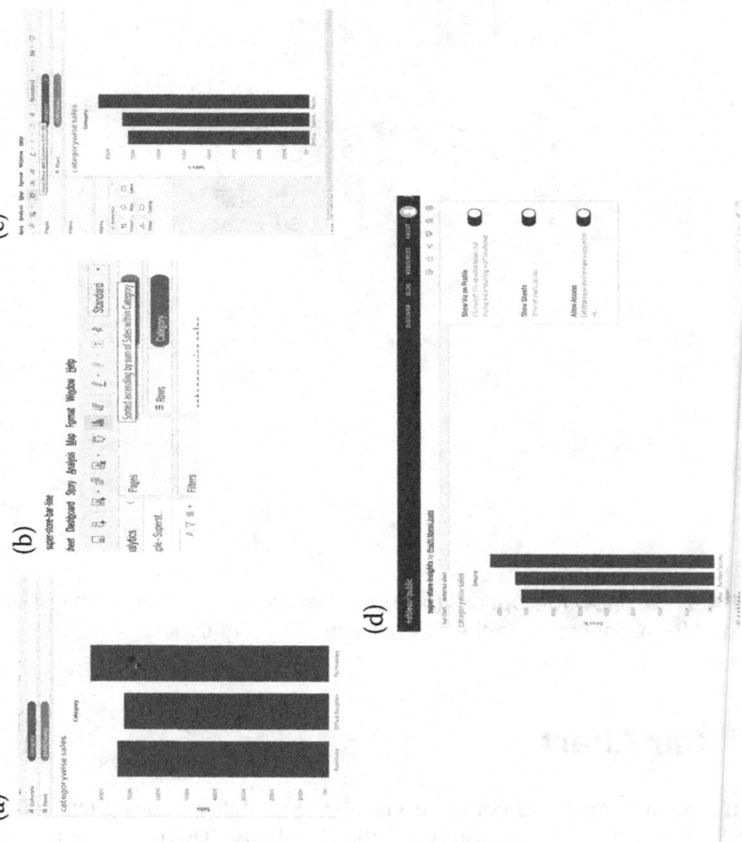

FIGURE 4.6 (a) Category Wise Sales – Bar Chart (b) Sorting Option – Ascending and Descending (c) Sorted, Row-column Swapped Bar Chart (d) Viz Published in Browser

1. Drag Category to Columns and Sales to rows.
   By default the bar chart gets generated.

The question addressed here is – What are the sales of each category overall?

Still, we have not explored the bar chart type options from Show Me. Let us use horizontal one from the Show Me. As one hovers on the options of the various chart type available in the Show Me, a tool tip below gets displayed which tells about the parameters and the type of chart with respect to dimensions and measures.

1. Simply duplicate the sheet by right clicking on the sheet.
2. Select horizontal bar to generate horizontal chart

Tip*: Click on the Show Me to hide the options, click it again to get the chart types.

While generating bar charts, audience would definitely prefer to see the things in a sorted order and for that, the viz can be sorted with use of ascending or descending options. Figure 4.6(b) shows the options and post-selection of ascending option along with swapping of rows and columns option, the visualization appears as in Figure 4.6(c). Before working further, rename the sheets, give captions and ensure to save the workbook by some name. The option available is 'Save to Tableau Public'. It will be saved on tableau Server and get published in browser. (Tableau may ask you sign in.) One would get a view as shown in Figure 4.6(d). Once your visualization is published, on the right side, refer Figure 4.6(d), settings turn on the options on show sheets. This will show all the generated visualizations. This published workbook is on your Tableau public profile.

To explore further options of bar charts, simply click the Show Me and check the options available. A different perspective to same question – **A stacked bar chart** is shown in Figure 4.7(a).

To generate it –

1. Duplicate sheet – the previous chart of Category and Sales – generated in Figure 4.6(a).
2. Select the stacked bar from Show Me
   Optional – drag and drop Category to Label in Marks card

Side-by-side bars can be used when we have to make comparative analysis. For example, the audience is interested to know the sales and profit comparison for each category of items.

To generate –

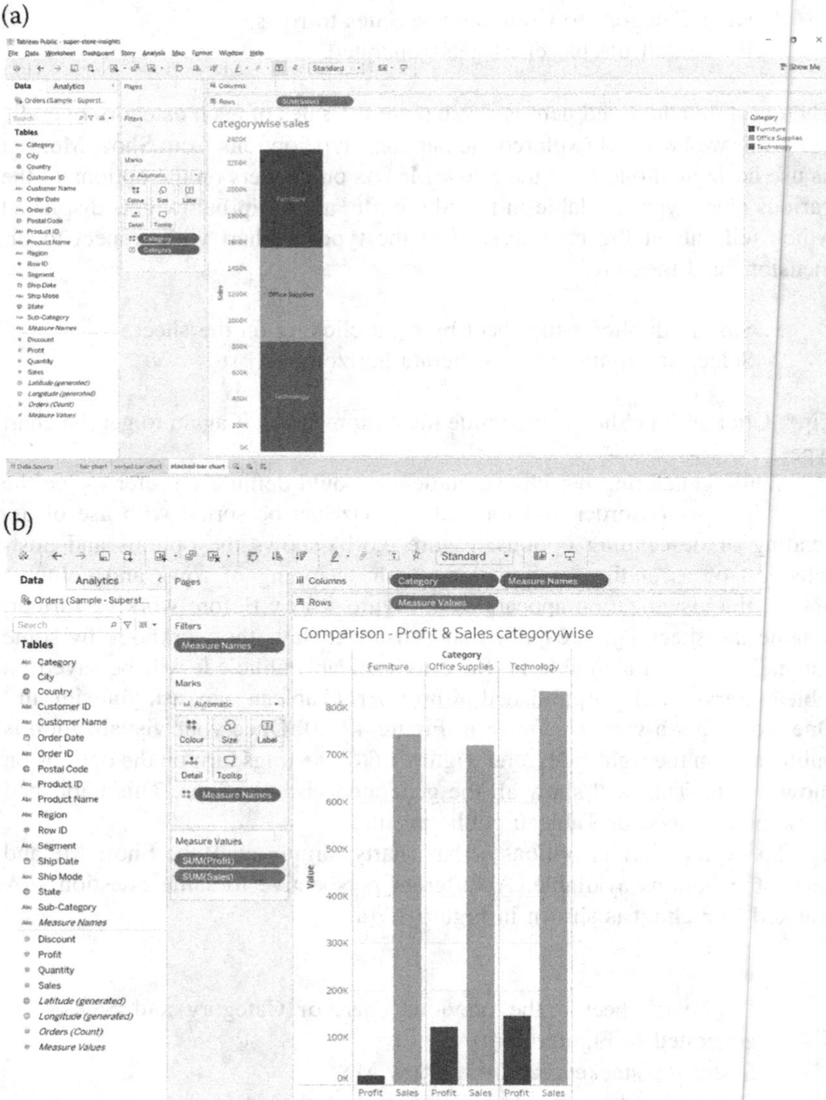

FIGURE 4.7 (a) A Stacked Bar Chart (b) Side-by-side Chart.

1. Duplicate the sheet – bar chart created in Figure 4.6(a)
2. Drag and drop Profit to rows
3. From Show Me – select side-by-side bar – Figure 4.7(b) is generated

Post selection of side-by-side bars, Tableau does some transformations that can be seen. One must have noticed the change in the color been made from the Marks card.

4.3.2 Line Charts

Line charts are used and recommended when a temporal variable is available. As discussed in Chapter 3, it is recommended when the audience is interested in knowing the trends over a period of time.

To generate a viz that shows the trend in sales for furniture category –

1. Drag and drop order date in columns and Sales in rows
2. Get Category in filters shelf and select Furniture

Figure 4.8(a) shows the viz generated.

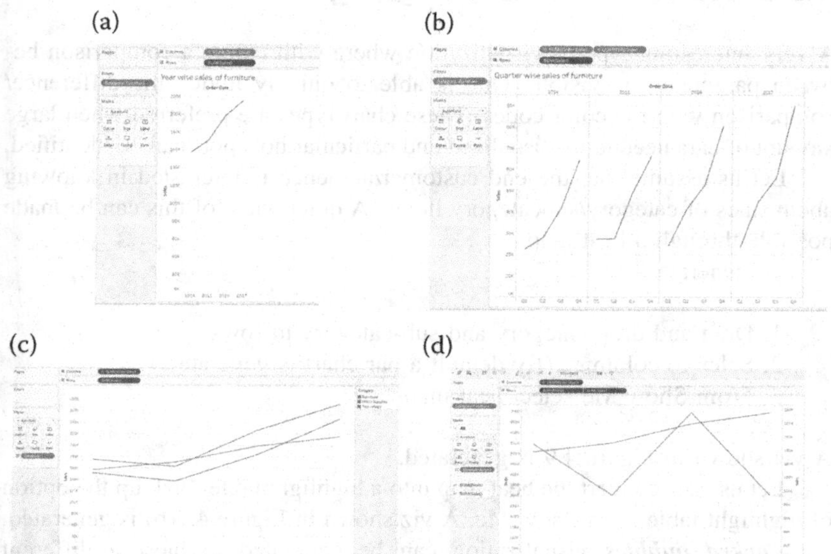

FIGURE 4.8 (a) Line Chart (b) Quarter-wise Sales for Furniture – Line Chart (c) Comparative Line Chart (d) Dual-line Chart – Sales and Profit.

Let us have another way of visualization. Imagine the audience – Sales manager/top-level management is interested in knowing the quarter-wise sales for four years. For this, click on the '+' at the year in the columns. A new pill – quarter gets added. A viz shown in Figure 4.8(b) is generated.

Likewise, one can go in detailing by clicking on the '+' for quarter and so on. To recover back the previous viz, simply drag it out i.e. remove the pill of quarter. This line chart is been generated for year, which is discrete. (Remember – blue color signifies it is discrete.)

Let us generate for continuous. Consider the line chart of Figure 4.8(a). From Show Me select lines (continuous). This will change the pill color of years to green and a line chart for this continuous parameter is generated. The way we generated the side-by-side bar chart, a **comparative line chart** can be generated to show comparison of sales for all three categories as shown in Figure 4.8(c). Use of Category here is in the color of Marks card. Going further, as an example consider the audience wants to know how sales and profit had the trend for furniture category. In such cases one can use 'dual lines' from Show Me. Figure 4.8(d) shows the use of same. Try to identify which parameters are been brought in which shelf/cards rows and columns.

4.3.3 Heat Maps and Highlight Tables

A very interesting type of visualization where with colors a comparison between parameters is visible. One is able to quickly notice the difference/comparison with the color codes. These chart types are preferred when large amount of data need to be visualized and particular hot spots can be identified.

Let us assume that the end customer/audience is interested in knowing about sales of category/subcategory items. A quick view of this can be made possible through a heat map.

To generate –

1. Drag and drop category and sub-category to rows.
2. Sales to columns. (By default a bar chart is generated.)
3. From Show Me select heat map.

A viz shown in Figure 4.9 is generated.

Let us now convert the heat map into a highlight table. Pick up the option of highlight table from Show Me. A viz shown in Figure 4.9(b) is generated.

Packed bubbles visualization can be generated to have a different lookout with respect to sales, though viz designers would prefer use of highlight tables or heat maps, these can be used with limited parameters and ensure that it is not cluttered (Figure 4.10(a)).

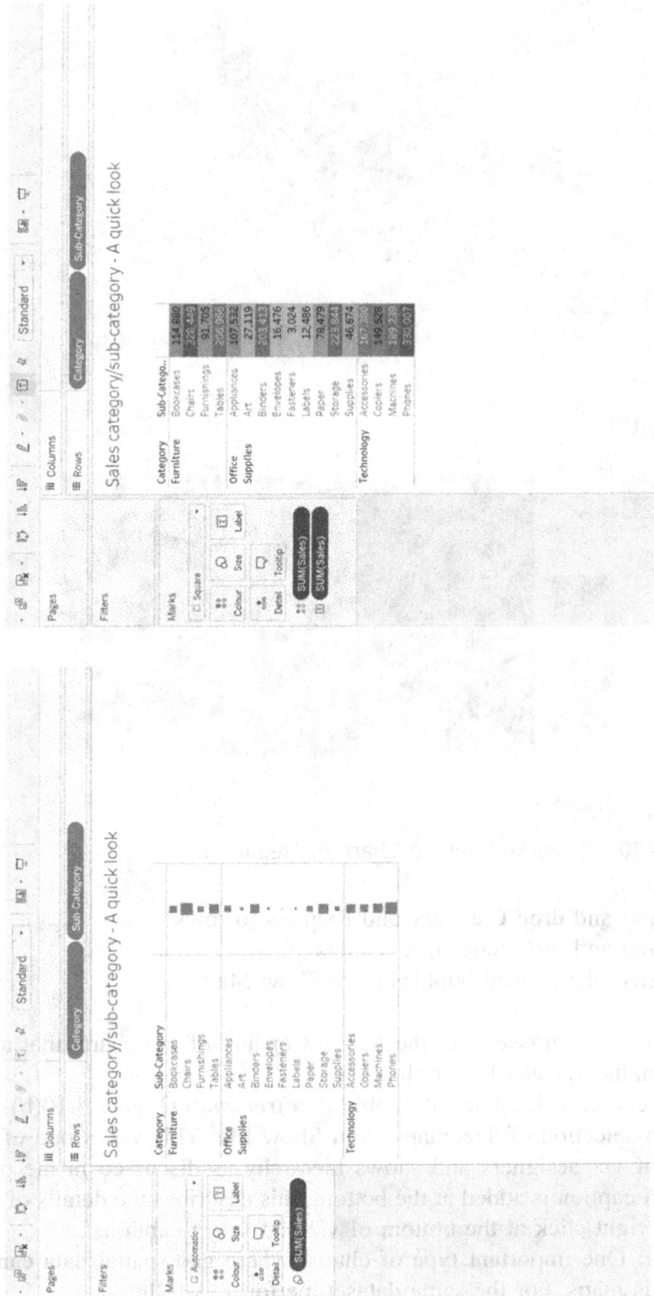

FIGURE 4.9 (a) Heat Map (b) Highlight Table.

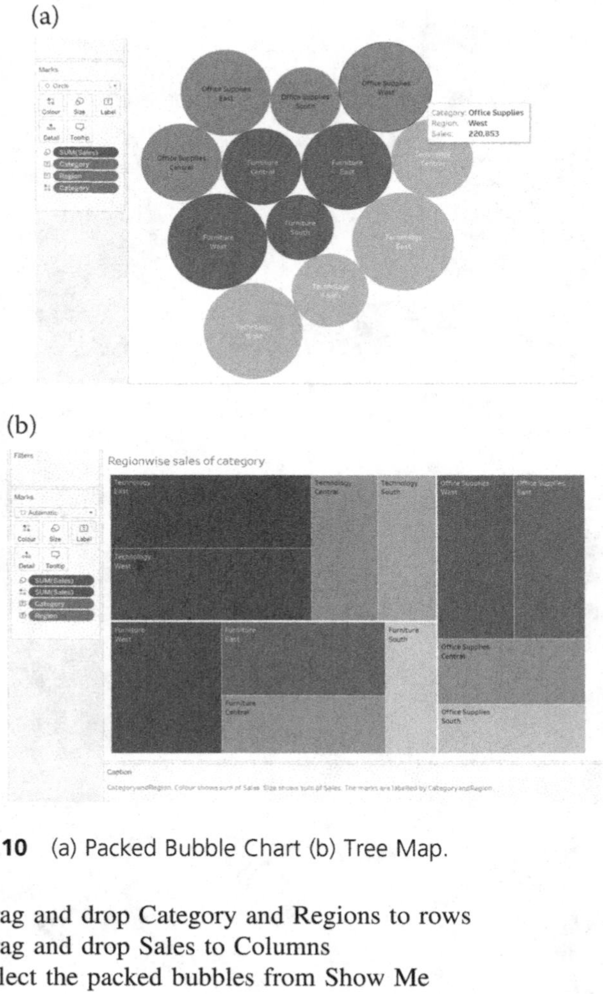

FIGURE 4.10 (a) Packed Bubble Chart (b) Tree Map.

1. Drag and drop Category and Regions to rows
2. Drag and drop Sales to Columns
3. Select the packed bubbles from Show Me

By hovering the mouse over the bubbles or any of the charts that are generated, details are seen like tooltip.

Conversion of the Packed bubble to a ***tree map*** (Figure 4.10(b)) can be done with selection of Treemaps from Show Me. This viz is one of the favourites of viz designers and shows hierarchy as discussed in the previous chapter. A caption is added at the bottom, this describes the details of the viz. To add – right click at the bottom of viz and select caption.

Maps: One important type of charts, where geo-spatial data can be visualized, is maps. For the same dataset, perform as follows:

1. Double click on Latitude and Longitude (these will automatically transfer to rows and columns)
2. Drag and drop Country and state to detail in Marks card.
3. Drag and drop Sales to color in Marks card.

Map is generated. The viz shows state-wise sales. (Similar to a highlight table) where the darker color shows maximum sales. Figure 4.11(a) depicts this visualization. (State is added to Label in Marks card as well.) To convert the map into ***symbolic maps***, Tableau provides Symbol maps, by which the same viz can be transformed to the one shown in Figure 4.11(b). The size of the circle can be varied from the Size in Marks card. ***Density maps*** discussed in the previous chapter can be obtained with –

(a)

(b)

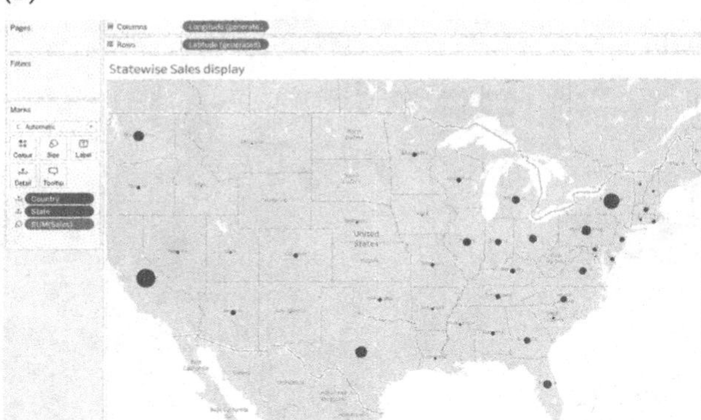

FIGURE 4.11 (a) Map – Sales State Wise (b) Symbolic Map – Sales State Wise.

i. Selection of density from the Automatic dropdown in Marks card.
ii. Further the color selection from the Marks card can make the viz look effective, thereby select special colors for intensity. Refer Figure 3.6(b). These maps serve purpose to show which area had highest sales.

Circles and side-by-side circles: This type of visualization is used when one is interested in having multiple dimensions added and they are to be visualized. What are region-wise category/subcategory items sales? This can be answered as follows:

1. Drag and drop Category, Subcategory and Region in columns.
2. Drag and drop Sales in rows. (By default, a bar chart is generated.)
3. Select circles view from Show Me. Viz in Figure 4.12(a) is generated.

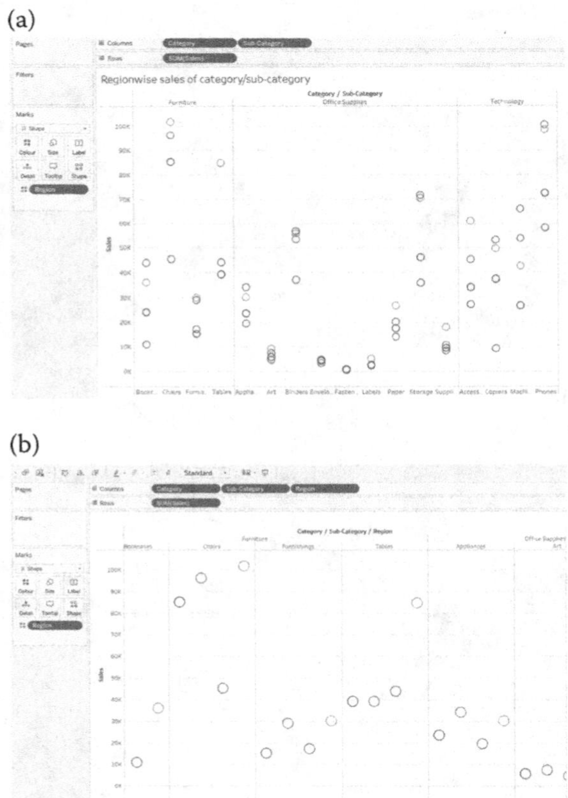

FIGURE 4.12 (a) Circle View (b) Side-by-side Circle's View.

Select Side-by-side circles from Show Me – a viz shown in Figure 4.12(b) is generated. Notice the difference in which the same data are displayed!!

These were few of the basic visualizations to make familiarity with Tableau. Readers can try with the remaining ones with different types of datasets and see if that visualization suffices the needs. Relate to the 'Right graph for right data' from Chapter 3.

4.4 CALCULATED FIELDS AND NULL VALUES

Tableau provides a feature to have calculated fields which can be used for having improved analytics and better visualizations. The calculated fields can be generated with inbuilt functions provided to deal with specific data types. It can be numeric or string. These calculated fields are often useful while dealing with null values. Consider dataset in Table 4.2.

Figure 4.13(a) shows a sample viz for the given dataset. The empty/blank values do not make the visualization effective – these are mapped to Null in viz. Moreover if the audience is interested in knowing about whether events are scheduled or not on particular dates, then a calculated field can help in dealing with this scenario.

1. Duplicating the event parameter
2. Edit the copy
3. Add a calculation – as shown in Figure 4.13(b)

TABLE 4.2 Dates with Associated Events

EVENT	*DATE*
Meeting in a Café	11-Oct
Lunch meeting with Mr. A	11-Oct
	12-Oct
Family get-together	13-Oct
	14-Oct
Golf	15-Oct
Team event	16-Oct

(a)

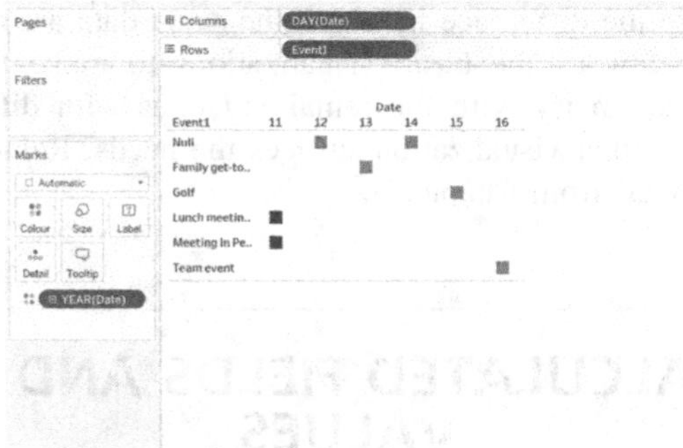

(b)

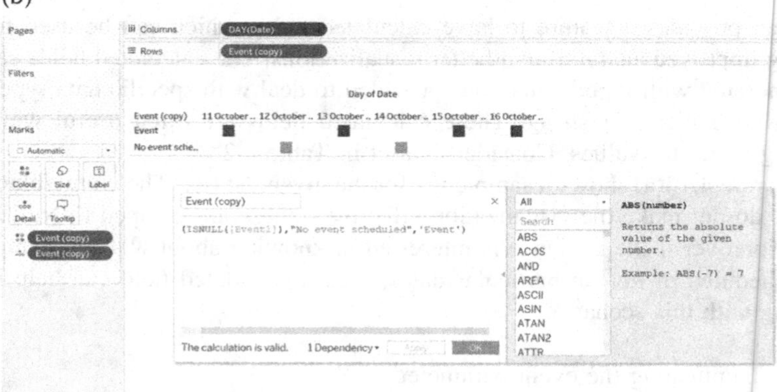

FIGURE 4.13 (a) Viz with Null Values (b) Viz – Mapping Null Values with Calculated Fields.

Notice the difference between the two visualizations generated. The calculated field can be generated in another way as well. Just right click on the data pane and create a calculated field. To deal with empty string, numerical data, different sets of functions are provided. For example, ZN, ISNULL and many more along with IF conditions to frame the calculation. The list of these functionalities can be seen in Figure 4.13(b). One more example can be assumed that a dataset comprising student details, marks, etc. is maintained. For some cases it could happen that the field of marks would have remained blank. Under these circumstances, one can map that field and put 0 or some minimum threshold value as desired. A simple calculation is: IFNULL([Marks], 0). The calculation will return the marks if not Null else will map it to zero.

4.5 INTERACTIVE DASHBOARD

It is time to get started with a dashboard creation! From the basic viz generation to bringing things on a dashboard makes the viz to start telling a story. The dashboard contains multiple charts that we created. Bringing them on dashboard makes them convey insights and at the same time making the dashboard an interactive one is a cherry on cake!! Though the decision to whether have an interactive dashboard or not solely depends on the requirements. A static dashboard if suffices the demands, one should not go for interactive dashboard. On the dashboard, one can add objects – images, links, text boxes and many more.

One can create a new dashboard from the menu or by selecting a new one next from bottom strip where sheets, dashboard and story can be added. Once this is created, the first step is to decide the layout of the dashboard. For this follow the following steps:

1. From the Dashboard pane on left, select Size drop down
2. Once can go for Fixed or Automatic.
3. If Fixed is selected, below this a drop down will appear from which one can select custom or a fixed page layout – A3, A4 and so on. Most of the times a fixed layout is preferred.

One more functionality with regard to this Dashboard creation is that of tiles and Floating. The way in which the objects are arranged on the dashboard varies with this selection. Readers can try this and see the difference.

To create interactive dashboard, we will use the same dataset of superstore and use the charts/viz we have already created. So, in the same workbook, we will create this interactive dashboard.

Step 1: Decide the layout (as discussed before).

Step 2: Bring the charts/viz required on the dashboard – drag and drop them. Arrange them as required. There is a dropdown named Standard below the menu bar. One can select as desired the layout of the respective chart from this. (Select Presentation mode next to the Standard dropdown – press F7 to see the view.)

With this a static dashboard is generated. One can add title, and other details as per requirement.

To have the dashboard interactive: Solution required for: A finance manager in the superstore wants to know about details of the sales and profit with respect to category as well as subcategory. The static dashboard can satisfy the demands. As an enhancement, manager can be presented with this interactive, where on selection of a specific category, the entire view of dashboard changes to the category selected thereby giving insights about the category specified.

To facilitate this, we have – (i) Bar chart of Sales against Category, (ii) Comparative chart of Sales and Profit for category, (iii) Highlight table of sales of sub-category – all three arranged on dashboard.

Note: While generating an interactive dashboard, there has to be a common parameter between the charts that you are bringing on dashboard.

In the case discussed, Category is a common parameter that exists in all the charts. The dashboard will show different visualizations as per selection of the category item.

So, let us convert this into an interactive one.

Step 3:

i. From the Dashboard menu select Action. A popup appears.
ii. On that popup, a drop down of Add Action is seen. Select it and select Filter option.
iii. From the Source Sheets select Bar chart and deselect the remaining two.
iv. Next to it 'Run action on'. Click the option of 'Select' from Hover, Select and Menu.
v. From the Target sheets select the remaining two charts and deselect the bar chart.
vi. Next to it is 'Clearing the Selection'. Select 'Show all values'. Budding designers can try all options.
vii. Click Ok.

We are ready with our interactive dashboard. Select Presentation View to experience this. Click on Furniture from the first bar chart and note the corresponding changes in remaining two charts with respect to this selection. Ensure to mention a tag indicating where the user should click so that this change in viz occurs. Figure 4.14(a) shows the Filter and 4.14(b) shows the interactive dashboard. The tag line is added below the heading in this dashboard.

A word of caution while creating dashboard – Do not bring too many charts on the dashboard and make it cluttered. It should be simple to understand and should not put cognitive load on the viewer. Also prefer static dashboard if the audience is not technology savvy and the basic demands can be showcased through a static viz.

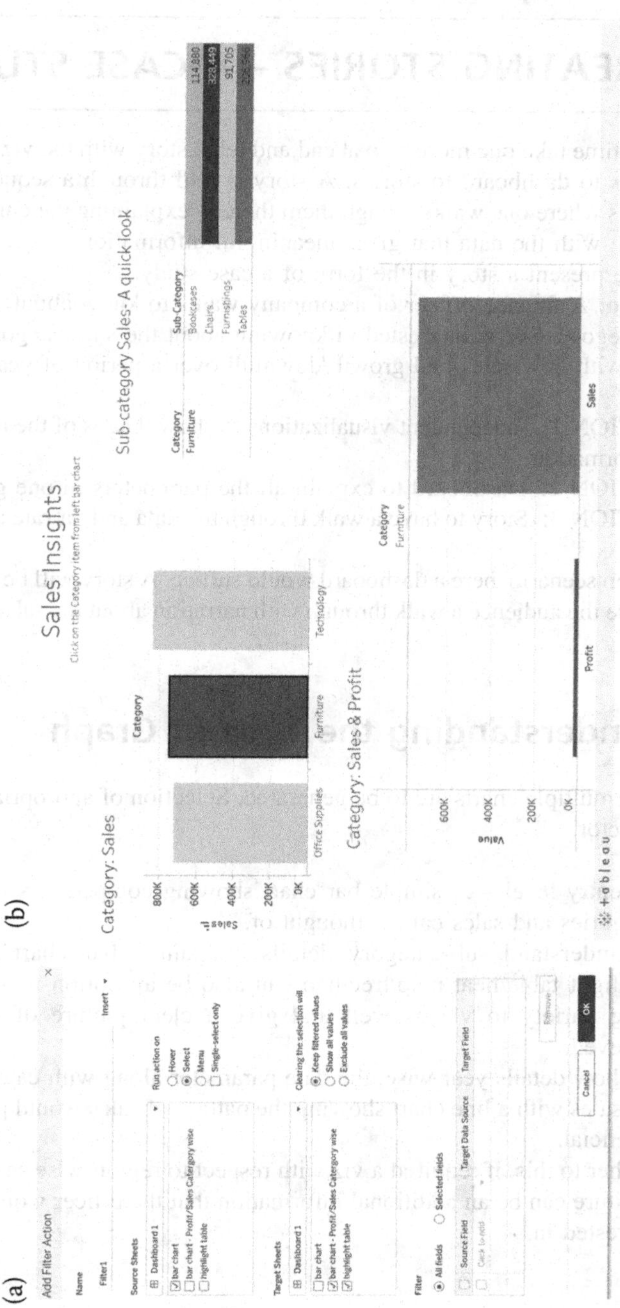

FIGURE 4.14 (a) Use of Filter (b) The Interactive Dashboard.

4.6 CREATING STORIES – A CASE STUDY

Finally, it is time take one more step ahead and tell a story with the viz – from simple charts to dashboard to stories. A story is told through a sequence of visualizations where one walks though them thereby explaining the context. It is a narration with the data that gives meaningful information.

Here we present a story in the form of a case study.

Scenario: A finance officer of a company wants to know about sales of furniture category. She is interested in knowing about the sub-category wise sales along with how sales had growth/downfall over a period of years.

SOLUTION 1: Independent visualizations to show details of the required information.
SOLUTION 2: Dashboard to explain all the parameters in one go.
SOLUTION 3: Story to have a walk through the data and narrate about it.

Depending on scenario, here a dashboard would suffice. A story will be a better option to give the audience a walk through with narration about the sales and its details.

4.6.1 Understanding the Type of Graph

In any case, multiple charts are to be generated. Selection of appropriate time is crucial factor.

1. For entry level – A simple bar chart showing comparisons of all categories and sales can be thought of.
2. To understand sub-category details – again a bar chart or a highlight table/heat map/treemap can also be an option that will bring variety to viz as well and give a clear picture of sales achieved.
3. To show details year wise, the date parameter along with category and sales with a line chart showing the pattern of sales would prove beneficial.
4. Further to this, if required a viz with respect to region-wise sales of furniture can be an additional information that the officer would be interested in.

(With the above set of viz, individual charts, interactive dashboard/static dashboard can be one of the solutions.) Let us explore with storyboard to showcase a better solution.

To generate a story –

i. Add new story
ii. Drag and drop new sheets/dashboard next to the caption button. New caption buttons will be generated and one is able to traverse through the sheets added.
iii. Ensure to give meaningful caption which will assist in the narration.

For the Scenario discussed, three viz are brought on the storyboard. Traversal, though the captions convey more about the viz and can be narrated with link to previous one. Figure 4.15 shows the story with individual sheets brought together on the storyboard. Each individual worksheet/dashboard that the story comprises is called a story point. Navigation through each story point tells a story about the data.

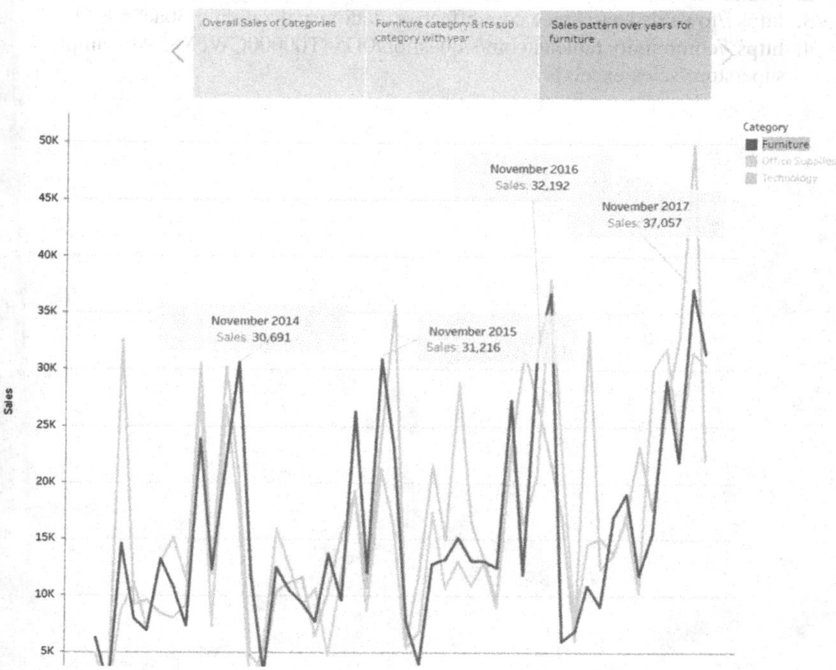

FIGURE 4.15 A Story of Furniture Sales.

4.7 CONCLUSION

The chapter brings out a platter of visualizations to explore in Tableau. Opening a new dimension for a novice viz designer, the chapter addresses how a viz can be generated. From a wide variety of graphs available, steps to bring out appealing and insightful viz are discussed. Dealing with null values to creation of a dashboard will make the reader understand the power of communicating data through visuals. Finally, a story of the data through viz makes the data more understandable and interpretable.

REFERENCES

1. www.tableau.com
2. Ben Jones, Communicating data with Tableau, O'Reilly, 2014.
3. https://towardsdatascience.com/effective-data-visualization-ef30ae560961
4. https://community.tableau.com/s/question/0D54T00000CWeX8SAL/sample-superstore-sales-excelxls

Conclusion 5

5.1 SUMMARY

This chapter concludes the book and proposes the future outlook which can be explored further to initiate new research avenues. This book intends to cover the big data analytics, its challenges, main building block of the data science i.e. data storytelling, communicating with data and storytelling context. Importance of visualization, its need, ethics and complete data visualization with Tableau is the main coverage of this book. Today, data storytelling and visualization have opened a new era for communicating meaningful insights. As we come to the conclusion on discussion of data storytelling and data visualization, the book brings out to the reader a bag full of visualizations to narrate a story and techniques to improve on the business intelligence.

The book, specially meant for novice designers, gives them a feel and understanding of how effective visualizations can be. The tremendous growth of data and the need to get vision and hidden information from them apparently makes it necessary to develop tools that will unleash the data. Tableau – one of the tools discussed – helps the readers to capture the essence of creating meaningful viz. Keeping in mind the requirements of audience and their personas are instrumental in making the visualizations. The book makes budding viz designer to consider these factors and emphasizes to be thoughtful in the process of viz creation. To summarize, it is all about bringing out right picture from the data to tell a story!!!

DOI: 10.1201/9781003307747-5

5.2 BUSINESS INTELLIGENCE

With the discussion on visualization, let us look at business intelligence (BI) relation to data storytelling and visualization. BI deals with analyzing the data that will make impact business decisions. BI is concerned with source data collection, transformation and then making some critical predictions. Now in this whole scenario, one can definitely say that the viz tools aid BI through visualizations. Though the visualizations created will be offering insights on the data, the capability that these tools posses would be a factor to set a boundary on the exploration of more powerful BI tools. BI can be explored with preliminaries of visualizations, analytics and thereby with narration of a story.

Internet of behaviours (IoB) is new emerging trend which deals with the identifying patterns from user's data which includes purchase patterns, usage pattern, watching history, etc. and then using this analysis to improve on the business. The success of IoB highly depends on how we make narratives from the given data and how we communicate with data as well as communicate data to the end users. In the sequel, fundamental hands-on approach on the data visualization using widely accepted visualization tools such as Tableau is the core component of this book. Step-by-step explanation of every aspect of visualization on the sample data set is explained in very lucid language in the scope of this book.

5.3 RESEARCH OPENINGS AND FUTURE OUTLOOK

Due to increasing data size and its increasing complexity, data-intensive research is going to be a major research area for next few decades. Data intensity comes with the pool of challenges and design issues especially in the context of research and development. As data science and data storytelling do not go alone, they should be linked to some use case so that appropriate dataset can be explored for the purpose of storytelling and analytics. The prominent research areas which can be explored further are as follows.

- Explainable artificial intelligence for driving use case
- Predictive analytics for preventive approach

- Data science for affective computing
- Storytelling and visualization for gamification
- Data exploration at edge computing
- Data exploration at fog computing
- Context aware proactive systems
- Sensor-Internet Sharing and Search
- Traffic characterization and classification
- Prescriptive analytics

In addition to this, there are other allied areas such as experimenting and validating data science techniques on real-time data posted on the cloud, mapping various machine learning techniques with respect to the nature and type of data set, proposing appropriate tools for cloud data analytics, etc. As a takeaway from the book, one must be motivated to look into futuristic opportunities in this world of viz and storytelling.

Index

Printed in the United States
by Baker & Taylor Publisher Services

Printed in the United States
by Baker & Taylor Publisher Services